On clichés

International Library of Sociology

Founded by Karl Mannheim

Editor: John Rex, University of Warwick

Arbor Scientiae
Arbor Vitae

A catalogue of the books available in the **International Library of Sociology** and other series of Social Science books published by Routledge & Kegan Paul will be found at the end of this volume.

On clichés

The supersedure of meaning by function in modernity

Anton C. Zijderveld
University of Tilburg, Netherlands

Routledge & Kegan Paul
London, Boston and Henley

First published in 1979
by Routledge & Kegan Paul Ltd
39 Store Street, London WC1E 7DD,
Broadway House, Newtown Road,
Henley-on-Thames, Oxon RG9 1EN and
9 Park Street, Boston, Mass. 02108, USA
Set in 10 on 11pt Times by
Kelly & Wright, Bradford-on-Avon, Wiltshire
and printed in Great Britain by
Redwood Burn Ltd,
Trowbridge and Esher

British Library Cataloguing in Publication Data

Zijderveld, Anton Cornelis

On cliches. – (International library of sociology).
1. Sociolinguistics 2. Communication
3. Terms and phrases
I. Title II. Series
301.14   P40   79-40448

ISBN 0 7100 0186 X

For Thomas, the definitive answer to all clichés

Contents

Preface

The present study is a specimen of what I have called elsewhere a 'cultural analysis'. The need for cultural analysis and its theoretical frame of reference has been discussed and explained in *The Abstract Society* (New York, 1970; London, 1973). If the reader wants to know 'what kind of sociology' the present study represents, he should consult this previous publication. Yet, a few explanatory – and, I am afraid, justifying – comments on this mode of sociological interpretation should still be made here. In order not to burden the reader with too long an introduction to the main argument of this book, I have decided to place them at the end in an appendix.

Clichés and their use in social and political life have always triggered my curiosity. It was, however, only after I had formulated the frame of reference of 'cultural analysis' as a continuation of so-called 'classic sociology' (Durkheim, Weber, Simmel, Mannheim, etc.), and in particular after I began to view clichés as phenomena which are not just linguistic by nature, that I was able to formulate the present sociological interpretation. Clichés are not only manners of speech which well-nigh coercively impose themselves on our linguistic efforts, but they are at the same time forms of thought, of action, and even of emotion which mould our thinking, acting and feeling in social life. I believe that clichés – like the traditional institutions of society, with which they have so much in common – can only be understood sociologically and discussed adequately in terms of 'cultural analysis'.

I am grateful to Peter L. Berger in New York who read an earlier draft of this study and who encouraged me strongly to finish it. Kurt Jonassohn and Michael Rosenberg, both of Montréal, and Anton Bevers in Nijmegen read the manuscript and made several valuable comments on it. The section on subjective and objective time in chapter 4 has benefited from discussions with Adrian C.

ix

Moulyn of Stamford, Conn., who already many years ago drew my attention to the sociological relevance of the problem of time.

Montréal-Tilburg   Anton C. Zijderveld

A speaker who uses that kind of phraseology has gone some distance towards turning himself into a machine. The appropriate noises are coming out of his larynx, but his brain is not involved as it would be if he were choosing his words for himself. If the speech he is making is one that he is accustomed to make over and over again, he may be almost unconscious of what he is saying, as one is when one utters the responses in church.

George Orwell, 'Politics and the English Language', 1946

Introduction

There are no white spots on our geographical maps any more. Every piece of the surface of the earth has been discovered and registered. For further explorations and discoveries we have to leave the earth and probe beyond the planets into the cosmos.

Could it be that by now the discovery of society,[1] which led to the emergence of sociology, has also been completed, and that as a result no major theoretical surprises are to be expected any more in this discipline? Is it possible that Marx's 'infra- and superstructure', Durkheim's 'social facts', Weber's 'social actions based on subjectively intended meanings', Simmel's 'forms of social life', Pareto's 'residues and derivations', Mannheim's 'social foundation of knowledge', Mead's 'meaningful interactions', Merton's 'manifest and latent functions', Parsons's 'social system' constitute the major theoretical continents of the sociological map? Could it be, in other words, that the task of sociological theory-construction, namely to fill up the white spots in our knowledge of socio-cultural reality, has in fact been completed and that consequently further developments of sociological theory will but consist of minor adjustments and additions – discoveries of little, relatively unimportant corners of social life? Could it be that from now on sociological theory will consist only of endless variations of the same themes and in particular of many repetitions? Can new, exhilarating discoveries within the field of theory, comparable to those of say Marx, Durkheim and Freud, still be expected in the social sciences and humanities in general? Is there still a sense of mystery, the awareness of yet unknown dimensions and facts, such as is the case in contemporary astrophysics which works with such fascinating conceptual conjectures as 'pulsars', 'quarks' and 'black holes'?

Isaac Asimov opens his book *The Collapsing Universe:The Story of Black Holes* (1977) with the following statement:[2]

1

Since 1960 the universe has taken on a wholly new face. It has become more exciting, more mysterious, more violent, and more extreme as our knowledge concerning it has suddenly expanded. And the most exciting, most mysterious, most violent, and most extreme phenomenon of all has the simplest, plainest, calmest, and mildest name – nothing more than a 'black hole'.

The discovery of society which by and large began at the end of the Middle Ages and gradually grew in breadth and scope during the process of modernization, leading up to the emergence of the sociological discipline in the nineteenth century, could of course never be as spectacular as recent discoveries in astrophysics apparently are. Society is to man what water is to a fish: it is difficult and it took quite some time to become consciously aware of this 'water' and to acquire systematic and rational knowledge about it.[3] However, the discovery and the ensuing theoretical and empirical explanations and interpretations of society seem to have been completed by now. Social reality does not seem to hide any mysterious 'black holes' and the sociological map seems to have no 'white spots' anymore.

If the further development of the socio-cultural sciences should indeed be devoid of any major surprises, we would be justified in assuming that socio-cultural reality itself has run out its course and will remain relatively unaltered and stable. Would it be too far-fetched indeed to view Western modernized civilization as a vast reservoir of cultural potentialities which by now have all been realized and explained? Could we not, as in a thought experiment, liken modern civilization to a computer programme, the variables of which have by now all been run off – realized in socio-cultural life, registered and analysed in socio-cultural sciences?[4] In such a state of entropy, culture would no longer yield new and vigorous styles and themes but linger on in unimaginative and repetitive neo-movements: neo-naturalism, neo-evolutionism, neo-primitivism, neo-classicism, neo-romanticism, neo-Marxism, neo-Hegelianism, neo-Freudianism, etc.[5] Can literature still produce a novel, music a symphony, art a sculpture or painting, social science a general theory without producing clichés? Restricting ourselves to the latter, are not the social sciences and humanities moulded in their styles of thought and in their themes of substantive research by cliché-producing neo-movements? Sociology, for instance, presents since roughly 1960 a bewildering array of mutually competing neo-movements. In a common attempt to end the predominance of neo-positivism which had so much characterized sociological research in the 1950s, sociologists began to return to Marxism and Freudianism, to phenomenology and existentialism and, since roughly 1970, to Wittgenstein's brand of analytic philosophy. Unavoidably, the result has been that the neo-positivist clichés of the 1950s were being substituted by clichés of a different methodological persuasion without really presenting a new perspective. They certainly did not constitute major theoretical discoveries, comparable to those made by Marx, Freud, Durkheim, Weber, or Simmel.

The late Arnold Gehlen once claimed that great theoretical discoveries are indeed no longer possible these days.[6] Darwinism, Marxism and Freudianism were the last socio-cultural and theoretical 'crystallizations'. According to Gehlen, further theoretical developments could but consist of minor adjustments and variations of these crystallizations. We live, he said, in a *post-histoire* in which no surprises are in store for us anymore. If Gehlen were right, we would just repeat old procedures and methods, pursue old aims and develop old themes. They only seem new to us, because our consciousness has increasingly become a-historical. We possess a very short memory and thus repeat old ideas and notions without actually realizing how worn-out and hackneyed they are.

Those of us who are still able to maintain an awareness of time and tradition, and who train ourselves in historical consciousness, are liable to be haunted by a continuous sense of *déjà vu* – a consciousness, incidentally, which in former days was the prerogative of the elderly members of society and which in modern society must necessarily appear as an arrogant relativism and irritating cynicism. In sociology Vilfredo Pareto was endowed with such a relativizing, historical awareness: he described the derivations as the hackneyed rationalizations of irrational residues. Pitirim Sorokin is another, more recent example. He obviously found great joy in confronting every contemporary socio-scientific 'discovery' with the wisdom of his *déjà vu*. Indeed, in the history of social thought, theorists like Pareto, Sorokin and Gehlen have always been extremely irritating and disconcerting. They will not easily turn into sources of clichés-producing neo-movements. Meanwhile, I fully realize that such rather pessimistic considerations are not very new and original either. In fact, the philosophy and mental attitude of *déjà vu* is as old as Ecclesiastes.[7] Moreover, such considerations are scientifically very questionable, to say the least. The notion of a civilization as a programme loaded with cultural potentialities which turn gradually into realities and then lose stamina and vigour, is actually only a version of the old organicist metaphor of cultures as life-cycles: they are born, grow up, have a vigorous adulthood, grow old and eventually die. Such metaphors usually served the by now rather hackneyed philosophies about a supposed decline of the West.

3

Yet, if one compares the obviously exhilirating socio-scientific discoveries of former days (Marx, Durkheim, Weber, Simmel, etc.) with the many neo-movements of today's sociology and its endless textbook repetitions of so-called 'classic' theories, if moreover one compares the contemporary sociological issues with the exhilirating mysteries yet to be solved in, for instance, biochemistry and astrophysics, one is compelled to draw the conclusion that either sociologists today are utterly unimaginative and unintelligent, or all major discoveries about socio-cultural reality have been made and have been theoretically registered and analysed. If I also see how other cultural sectors, such as art, literature and music, are presently dominated by countless neo-movements and their epigones, I am strongly inclined to explain the present state of sociology (and of the other social sciences and humanities as well) not in terms of intellectual deficiency on the part of sociologists, but in terms of cultural entropy. The problem itself then becomes a sociological problem.[8]

There is, however, as far as I can see, no way to directly attack this problem of cultural entropy scientifically. In fact, one very easily ends up in metaphysical conjectures and rather sultry theories of cultural pessimism. In this study I try to tackle the issue in a more indirect and circumspect manner by limiting myself to one single phenomenon: the social and political functions of clichés in fully modernized societies. I shall not be able to empirically prove the existence of cultural entropy but the speculative notion of such an entropy did very much steer my attention to the cliché as a sociological phenomenon in modern society. I find it to be a matter of methodological honesty to put this metaphysical trump card on the table right at the start of this book.

After having defined and described the cliché sociologically in terms of the supersedure of meaning by function, the present study will try to demonstrate how modernization (a collective term for processes such as industrialization, urbanization, secularization, rise of capitalism and bureaucracy, etc.) strongly fosters the use of clichés in human speech, thought, emotion, volition and action. It will be argued at the same time that the clichés form the main components of modern consciousness and thus foster modernity (a concept referring to the mentality and the ethos of a modernized society). It is hoped that such a sociological theory of the cliché will reveal some hitherto undetected dimensions of modernization and of modernity.

In the history of human civilization we can discover two socio-cultural contexts which strongly foster the functioning of clichés. Prior to modernization we find such a clichégenic context, when in a society religion and religious explanations of the world are totally

4

subdued to magic and magical manipulations of reality. The second clichégenic context can be found in fully modernized societies in which, due to many sociological factors, meaning has been increasingly superseded by function. In these two contexts of which the second will be primarily discussed in this book, human speech in daily conversations and in various reality interpretations (either mythical or scientific), creative activities in art, literature and music, various activities related to policy (from 'primitive' war raids to 'modern' political diplomacy) tend to follow routine paths and traditional patterns. That is, they are moulded by clichés which tend to hold a firm grip over the individual's consciousness.

In both socio-cultural contexts, individuals tend to take the clichés of their society for granted. They have been passed on from generation to generation (tradition) acquiring the status of naturalness and normalcy through the process of socialization. As superficial as they may seem to be, clichés are generally deeply installed in man's consciousness where they can do their work, as we will see later, without the interference of potentially relativizing reflections. Usually, individuals are rather apprehensive about any form of critique or relativization of their clichés, they seem to cut deeply into their emotional life. The modern scientist, for example, watches over the axioms and tenets of his 'paradigm', just as the pre-modern priest guards his doctrines and pre-modern magician hides his secret formulas – this notwithstanding the scientist's lofty principle of falsification. Indeed, shaking up a society's clichés is as hazardous an enterprise as trying to overthrow its institutions.

Societies which follow the path of modernization – and almost all societies on earth sooner or later will have to follow this path – will unavoidably become clichégenic. There is, as chapter 2 will argue, an elective affinity between modernity and the tyrannical reign of clichés. Daily speech, for example, tends to lose its substance of meaning when a society modernizes. As a result, the art of conversation is increasingly forgotten. Instead, modern man has become a virtuoso in chatter, as is clearly demonstrated in so-called party chit-chat and by the remarkable phenomenon of the television talk-show. Likewise, the art of letter writing has rapidly declined during the rise of modernization and the ensuing developments of tele-communication: rather than taking the time to carefully compose a letter, modern man picks up the telephone and chats. In this chatter there is no room for reflection: speech is conveniently moulded according to hackneyed patterns of thought and verbal expression, and so are the accompanying thoughts and emotions. It makes our communications efficient and easily (i.e. pre-reflectively) understandable.

The most remarkable feature of clichés lies in their capacity to by-

5

pass reflection and to thus unconsciously work on the mind, while excluding potential relativizations. When people reflect upon a statement, they will think about its content of meaning, and weigh its worth and value. This entails an element of relativization, since the content of meaning of the statement is no longer taken for granted and accepted on face value. Clichés manage to avoid this relativization brought about by reflections. By means of sheer repetition clichés mould people's minds and souls in a specific direction. This effect is reinforced by the fact that clichés are almost as contagious and catching as laughter. Just because reflection is, as it were, put aside, both laughter and clichés are easily imitated. Yet, as we will argue later, clichés do work on the mind. They do influence people on the attitudinal level and it is precisely for this reason that clichés are so much used in politics and commerce (cf. political and commercial slogans).

As is often the case when one becomes aware of a phenomenon which was hitherto taken for granted, the cliché seems to be ubiquitous in modern society. Wherever we are – in our living room at home, or in the office at work, in the university lecture room, or in the hospital room at occasions of birth or of death, of marriage or of divorce – clichés seem to roll ever so easily over our tongues, moulding our thoughts, emotions, volitions and actions. Indeed, we exchange clichés like the many coins of our inflated economic system. They are easily coined and as easily spent, and they are available in great quantities. Fowler, that astute linguistic observer, was right when he circumscribed clichés as 'convenient reach-me-downs' that can be taken off the peg and used mechanically, whenever we need them.[9]

The present study sets out to develop a sociological theory of the cliché. It might well be the only chance left to take a sociological revenge on the tyranny by which clichés rule consciousness· and society today. This revenge, however, can only have the character of an exposure. As will be argued throughout this study, human beings can never dispose of clichés, we need them for our daily interactions and for the functioning of society at large, as much as we need the institutions. This ambiguity will be the *Leitmotif* of the following discussion.

1 Clichés defined

The supersedure of meaning by function

Introduction

Since the industrial revolution began in England and the ensuing process of modernization received its greatest impulses in the USA, the English language has become the *lingua franca* of modernity. Prior to the modernization of Europe and the USA, French held this position, as the term *lingua franca* seems to indicate. It was in particular the international language of the European monarchies and nobilities (which it, apparently, still is) and of the higher bourgeoisie (as, for instance, in czarist Russia). Even today there are still quite a few French words and concepts which seem to defy translation into English: *in lieu, milieu, vis-à-vis, bourgeoisie, rendez-vous, risqué, élite*, etc. They are the linguistic remnants of a bygone age. Significantly, the word *cliché* as both noun and adjective belongs to this linguistic category.

The word cliché referred originally to a cast or dab by which pictures could be massively reproduced in a relatively easy, fast, and thus economical procedure. As such the cliché stood, together with the invention of typography, at the cradle of modern technology, and contributed to the rise of modernity. *The Oxford English Dictionary* provides a terse definition of this original meaning of the word cliché: 'a cast obtained by letting a matrix fall face downward upon a surface of molten metal on the point of cooling, called in English type-foundries "dabbing".'[1] The word has later been extended to the negative in photography. In the world of printing the synonym stereotype is for obvious reasons often used.

It is rather remarkable that the famous Oxford Dictionary discusses the widely spread metaphorical meaning of cliché only very briefly in its supplement: 'a stereotype expression, a commonplace phrase.'[2] *The Random House Dictionary of the English Language*

7

is much more elaborate and thus more helpful. It defines a cliché as '1. a trite, stereotyped expression; a sentence or phrase, usually expressing a popular or common thought or idea that has lost originality, ingenuity and impact by long overuse, as "sadder but wiser", or "strong as an ox". 2. (in art, literature, drama, etc.) a trite or hackneyed plot, character development, use of color, musical expression, etc. 3. (a) a stereotype or electrotype plate, (b) a reproduction made in a like manner.–adj. 4. trite; hackneyed, stereotyped; commonplace.'[3]

The same dictionary mentions as synonyms: platitude, bromide, stereotype, commonplace. It distinguishes, however, s.v. commonplace, between the following kindred concepts: commonplace refers mainly to dull ordinary, platitudinous thought; banal refers to what seems to be inane, insipid, and pointless; hackneyed suggests – very much like cliché – something stale and worn out by overuse; stereotyped suggests the notion of repetitive similarity, to such an extent as to seem automatic; trite, very much like cliché, refers to something which was originally striking, but has become well known and overused, as in 'true but trite'.[4] The synonyms closest to cliché thus are the adjectives 'hackneyed' and 'trite'. The origin of the first is sociologically quite interesting. The Oxford English Dictionary relates, s.v. hackney, that the word originally meant a horse which was neither a war horse, nor a hunter nor a draught horse, but a horse (primarily for ladies) to pleasantly ride. It also meant quite early a horse for hire and a prostitute. The second synonym is derived from the Latin tritus, meaning worn and common. Originally trite referred to 'rubbed, or worn by use' and then became used as synonym of hackneyed and stale.[5]

As the original meaning of cliché indicates, this phenomenon entered the orbit of Western civilization as a piece of early industrial technique, as a rational procedure to quickly and massively reproduce cultural material. Illustrations which prior to the invention of typography were carefully and often painstakingly drawn and painted (cf. the often magnificent illuminations in medieval manuscripts), could now be reproduced quickly and massively. These clichés can be stored away and they can, in principle, produce illustrations whenever one needs them. Such reproductions may often lack the charm and meaningful uniqueness of those medieval hand-painted illuminations, but they have the advantage that they can be attached time and again to printed words and made available to large quantities of readers. That is, compared to those illuminations, although these stereotyped pictures may have lost meaning and aura, they have definitely gained in functionality. It will be argued in this chapter that this supersedure of meaning by function is much more pertinent still in the hackneyed, overused and stale expressions which we metaphorically also call clichés.

8

A sociological definition

The definition of the cliché which I shall give in this section does not pretend to tell the reader what a cliché actually or essentially is. I do not believe in such 'essentialism'. The definition rather suggests how one could look *sociologically* at a phenomenon which belongs to our daily communications and which the dictionary happens to call 'a cliché'. What this phenomenon 'essentially' and 'in and for itself' is, I do not and cannot know. However, after I have become reflectively aware of it and after I have read the lexicographical descriptions in the dictionary, I can make an effort to describe, define and analyse it sociologically.

Although this is strictly speaking not necessary, it does help to start a sociological treatise as the present one with a definition that sums up the major sociological characteristics of the phenomenon. Such a sociological definition tries to comprehensively formulate the 'sociological essence' of the cliché. This is, of course, not essentialism but 'perspectivism': the cliché is described, defined and interpreted through the perspective of the sociological discipline.

However, there is not one perspective of a uniform sociological discipline. Sociology knows different theoretical and methodological approaches each of which sheds its own light on reality. I have chosen one such approach and I should at least briefly indicate its nature.

By and large the present sociological definition and ensuing arguments have been strongly influenced by G. H. Mead's social psychology which has later received the name 'symbolic interactionism'. I chose this perspective not because I am a 'symbolic interactionist' but because I believe that Mead's theoretical approach to social reality yields a perspective which is best suited to define, describe and analyse a phenomenon like the cliché.

There is, I think, a remarkable convergence between Mead's notion of meaningful, social interaction and Weber's notion of social action based on subjectively intended meaning, as well as between Mead's concept of the 'generalized other' and Durkheim's concept of the 'collective/consciousness conscience'. The conceptual bridge between the Weberian and Durkheimian approaches to social reality was found by Mead, when he launched the notion of 'taking the role of the other': by taking the role of the generalized other, individual action and consciousness are tied to collective action and consciousness. The result is a socio-psychological theory of interactions and institutions which has been theoretically elaborated by Peter L. Berger and Thomas Luckmann in *The Social Construction of Reality* (New York, Doubleday, 1967). In sum, the theoretical and methodological frame of reference of the sociological approach that has been chosen here should not be viewed in terms of American 'symbolic interactionism'. It is rather founded on some of the original notions and concepts of Mead which are being tied to some basic tenets of 'classic', European sociology of knowledge.

I fully realize how pedantic it is to start with a formal definition and then to elaborate one's theoretical arguments. Not rarely, trite theories are the result of such pedantry. However, while working on the manuscript of this book, I discovered how complex the phenomenon that I wanted to understand better really is, and how easy it is to drift off into vague and hazy abstractions. A definition can assist in an orderly and clear elaboration of one's arguments, but the structure it imposes on one's observations and interpretations can become a strait-jacket, leaving too little room to manoeuvre theoretically. It also can function as a guide, keeping the theorist on the road. I have tried to construct a definition which can function in the second sense:

> A cliché is a traditional form of human expression (in words, thoughts, emotions, gestures, acts) which – due to repetitive use in social life – has lost its original, often ingenious heuristic power. Although it thus fails positively to contribute meaning to social interactions and communication, it does function socially, since it manages to stimulate behaviour (cognition, emotion, volition, action), while it avoids reflection on meanings. *Summary*: The sociological essense of a cliché consists of the supersedure of original meanings by social functions. This supersedure is caused by repetitive use and enhanced by the avoidance of reflection.

We shall first discuss point-by-point the main elements of this definition. The concepts of meaning and function will be covered separately in the next section together with the dynamics of supersedure. The latter will be further elaborated in chapter 2. It is the very pivot of our argument. The social functions, mentioned in the definition, will be extensively discussed in chapter 3.

1   The definition speaks of the cliché as a form of human expression which belongs to tradition. As in the case of a joke, it is in most cases very hard, if not impossible to determine when, where and by whom a cliché was originally coined. Strictly speaking, clichés are not coined. They have gradually, through repetitive use sometimes by several generations, become part and parcel of cultural tradition, and acquired the coercive power of institutions. We return to this point presently and focus now on the formal and traditional nature of the cliché only.

10

When the expression was originally coined and had not yet become trite and hackneyed, it related in a spirited and ingenious manner some experience and observation of reality. Shakespeare has always been a rich source of clichés. He formulated many witty and spirited statements about human beings and socio-cultural circumstances which, because of their overuse, have become rather stale and worn-out clichés: 'to be or not to be', 'method in madness', 'there is something rotten in the state of - - - -', etc. When Shakespeare coined them, these expressions still had semantic power. They still spelt an ingenious and spirited vision of reality; when we use them, they have lost all heuristic and semantic pith, and do no longer testify to any ingenuity or originality. Yet, as we will see in more detail later, they do function socially.

In sum, we could view clichés, perhaps a bit crudely, as containers of old experiences. They contain, in a sense, the experiences and observations of former generations, were once spirited, ingenious and original but have now grown stale and common through repetitive overuse. Clichés contain the stale wisdom of past generations – elements of the 'collective consciousness' of yester-year. This wisdom is an institutional part of tradition and is carried over from generation to generation by clichés. If this wisdom has lost its original semantic power and heuristic pith, if it no longer helps us to understand better man and socio-cultural reality, it still helps us in a more functional manner: it can, in cliché form, help us to influence and stimulate consciousness and behaviour, without the relativizing interference of reflection.

2   The primary connotation of a cliché is linguistic: we view a cliché first of all as an overused, wornout statement or sentence – a phrase which has lost its semantic vigour. For example, a phrase like 'the home is where the heart is' might still be genuinely touching to a foreigner not well versed in the English tongue; to native English speakers in the USA and Britain it has long since lost its semantic pith and has become a rather corny cliché.

But clichés transcend these linguistic parameters. A silent gesture can become a cliché, like the Western European shaking of hands, or men kissing each other's cheeks in Eastern Europe. Such gestures are not to be taken literally. Indeed, they don't mean a thing. They are merely functional in the daily routine. Likewise, a more complex act like students occupying a university building in the 1970s can easily be viewed as a cliché. The original, expressive and symbolic meaning of this act which stirred genuine emotions and reflections in the 1960s, has grown stale in the 1970s. Today, the announcement of such an occupation is received rather laconically in terms of a bored sense of *déjà vu*, even by the mass media. It might still be

functional to the aims of the organizers, but it has definitely lost its
original symbolic value and meaning – it has become a cliché. To
give still another example of a non-linguistic cliché, it is very hard
these days to restore the original, ideological flavour and enthusiasm
of the early labour movement during a strike. The act of an industrial strike has long since become a cliché: it has lost much of its
symbolic vigour, while it has gained, as we all know, quite a lot of
political functionality. A strike is a rational and legally arranged
means in the hands of labour leaders to realize the goals of their
unions.

In sum, clichés do not consist exclusively of words, statements,
phrases and slogans ('power to the people', 'black is beautiful', etc.),
but also of gestures (a functional shaking of hands) and acts (an
occupation, a strike). The essential feature is in all cases the change
from symbolic vigour and semantic power, to social and/or political
functionality – a supersedure of meaning by function.

3 Because of the originally expressive and symbolic nature of
clichés, they are liable to occur rather massively in art, literature
and music. In drama, for instance, a plot like that of *Romeo and
Juliet* has long since become a cliché, gratefully adopted by the
cinema. A character role like the tragic jester, like the hero of
Rigoletto or the sad clown, has also turned into a (often rather corny)
cliché. Generally, it is the function of these aesthetic clichés to
enable people to consume and digest artistic products in a leisurely
fashion and without much reflection. The novels of Hedwig Courts-
Mahler in Germany, for example, which have lately regained
popularity in Europe, were all characterized by clichéd plots,
characters, emotions and thoughts. Likewise, the once very popular
Warsaw Concerto, composed by putting together many Rachmaninov
and Tchaikovsky clichés, was obviously geared towards an unproblematic, aesthetic consumption which would yield a massive,
commercial profit. Such cliché-ridden art, music and literature,
whose aim it is to present easily consumable and commercially
profitable products, is called *kitsch*. (We shall see in the next chapter
that this observation can also be reversed: in a society which is
economically based on commercialization and mass consumption
the arts will be put under heavy stress to produce clichés and
kitsch.)

4 Clichés can be easily consumed because they do not require
cognitive reflection. (As was said in the Introduction, this feature of
clichés is extremely important to our whole argument. It is the very
pivot of the functionality of clichés. We will return to this point
later, but must briefly mention it here.)

Most clichés are able to trigger speech and behaviour in a kind of behaviouristic stimulus–response mechanism. In speech, for example, a cliché is easily and without the interference of any thought, taken over – just as one must in fact consciously watch one's own tongue when speaking with someone who stutters badly. Or to use still another comparison, clichés are as contagious as laughter. In all these cases, cognitive reflections remain as it were in the background of the interaction. But clichés, on the contrary, do not stand in the background: they are so to say ready-to-be-used. It only needs specific words to trigger them off. This is very much the case, as Fowler has observed, with certain adjectives which are almost automatically attached to certain nouns:[6]

> There are thousands for whom the only sleep is the 'sleep of the just', the light at dusk must always be 'dim, religious'; all beliefs are 'cherished', all confidence is 'implicit', all ignorance 'blissful', all isolation 'splendid', all uncertainty 'glorious', all voids 'aching'.

Fowler calls them correctly 'associated reflexes'. We must, however, probe deeper. Because of their repetitive use in social life, people will not think much about the precise meaning of a cliché, yet they will hear it and incorporate it into their ongoing interactions. It is my contention that clichés thus manage unobtrusively to penetrate into man's consciousness and to influence behaviour on the attitudinal level, while potential relativizations are being excluded because cognitive reflections are being avoided. Clichés thus bring people unobtrusively into a certain mood. They mould their mentality and attitude, and thus gradually prepare them to speak, to think, to feel and act in a specific direction. This direction is not clearly indicated by the cliché but by the wider semantic context in which it is used. For example, when a politician talks repetitively about his and our 'democratic duties', the cliché adjective 'democratic' is used in order to mould our political attitudes and inclinations in the direction of this particular politician's party and platform. In like manner function such clichés as 'God–given right', 'freedom', 'our nation' and 'order'. The individual members of the politician's audience are not supposed to reflect on the meanings of these concepts. Instead they are being used over and over again, and the intention is to thus mould the political attitudes and inclinations of potential voters into a specific political direction. Commercial and religious clichés function in precisely the same manner. It is a kind of brainwashing, and in order to be successful, a rather crass kind of behaviourism has to be applied: the cliché as stimulus has to be repeated over and over again in order to achieve the thoughtless, mechanical response it set out to elicit. Clichés resemble

13

food that is easy to swallow and easy to digest, as it were without much chewing.

In sum, clichés are no longer symbols but have become signals which trigger off speech and behaviour as if they were reflexes. These reflexes prepare people's mood and attitude. When, in a rather long speech, someone says: 'last but not least', nobody in the audience is supposed to think, let alone ask: 'if not least, why not first?' The cliché does in fact not say what it says. It is a rather overworked expression signalling that the speech is finally coming to its long awaited conclusion. It might have been full of ideas whose meaning the audience had tried to understand reflectively – the spoken words being taken as meaningful symbols. But the remark 'last but not least' had no symbolic meaning to be pondered reflectively; it functioned merely as a signal heralding the end of the speech in a rather unimaginative manner. Not rarely, this cliché is used as a last effort to keep the audience's attention; the reflex it often triggers is a slight sigh of relief.

5   Since their meaning is irrelevant, clichés often consist of very brief interjections, or of vocal and bodily gestures. One of the most inflated clichés of the English language is the interjection 'you know'. Taken literally, these two words have a clear meaning, but used as an interjection – very often in every second sentence – they lose all semantic content. In fact, these two words have become so meaningless that they – in terms of clichés – represent a border case: in many speakers they seem to be a substitute for stuttering. In any case, the response 'no I don't know' or 'yes I might know' is obviously totally out of place. This cliché rather tries to instil in the person addressed the feeling that he should agree with the speaker – an unconscious attempt to bring about consensus. If these words are interjected repetitively, the reflection 'I am not sure, if that is correct' does not get a chance to arise in the mind of the addressed person; he is unobtrusively coerced into following the speaker.

Many such interjections are emotionally neutral: 'as far as I am concerned', 'incidentally', 'by the way'. They roll easily off the tongue and enter as easily into the ears of those to whom we speak. There are, however, also interjections which are emotionally expressive: 'oh my!', 'good grief!', 'oh, oh!' (with a tone difference of a third), 'come on now!', 'hey, man!' Maybe such interjections do send out messages belonging to a sort of 'meta-talk'.[7] However, it needs some heavy psycho-analytic assumptions to really maintain that kind of interpretation. In any case, these interjections remain semantically rather thin, lacking meaning, yet influencing people on the attitudinal level. They create a mood, they mould a mentality, and since they are used repetitively in daily interactions, people will not even notice them reflectively which further enhances their functionality. In this respect, interjections are typically clichés.

6 Clichés and slogans have much in common, yet they are not necessarily the same. A slogan is a catchy phrase or dictum, meant to mobilize people to buy a product, to vote for a particular political programme, or to believe in one or another world-view or ideology. Clichés share this mobilizing function, but they are yet primarily characterized by the fact that they have lost their original ingenuity, their original semantic vigour and heuristic pith, due to a repetitive overuse in daily social life. As a result, clichés are not catchy anymore. In fact, Muzafer Sherif suggested that slogans may well function 'to revive or strengthen an already well-established stereotype'.[8] That is, in some cases slogans may be consciously devised in in order to revive the original meaning and ingenuity of worn-out clichés.

However, we should add to this that slogans in their turn may also develop into clichés, when used repetitively and subjected to the previously mentioned inflation of meaning. 'The family that prays together, stays together', 'United we stand, divided we fall', 'Better Red than dead' (or the other way about) are obvious examples.

There is a sociologically significant difference between clichés and slogans. While clichés are like the coins of an inflated monetary system, constantly and mindlessly exchanged in daily social life, this is rarely the case with slogans. The catchy phrases of the commercials to which television viewers are so frequently exposed, are very rarely used in daily social intercourse. Generally, commercial, political and religious slogans do not become part of the semantic currency of daily social life. However, if this does happen, as was the case with the famous Kennedy phrase of the 1960s – 'Don't ask what America can do for you, ask what you can do for America' – repeated *ad nauseam*, even far outside the political arena, slogans indeed tend to turn into clichés.

7 Let us now turn our attention to a different dimension of the cliché. Within language and social behaviour in general, clichés can be set apart as distinct entities. That is, they have a reified nature. As we have seen, clichés are the containers of past experiences. It is the dimension of reification which further substantiates that fact.

Clichés do not belong to what William James called our 'stream of consciousness': they are not part of the ever changing and evolving experience of time which Henri Bergson termed '*durée*'. On the contrary, clichés are well-nigh lapidary chunks of stale experience.

15

Because of their reified nature, clichés can be collected like stamps or, even better perhaps, like jokes. Eric Partridge, the skilled collector of such other linguistic pebbles as slang and catch phrases, published a *Dictionary of Clichés* (New York, 1966), while H. W. Fowler adds a small selection of clichés to his article on 'hackneyed phrases'.[9] Much of the fun of reading Nierenberg and Calero's previously mentioned book *Meta-Talk* lies precisely in the fact that they wittily analysed the many clichés which we all mindlessly use in daily social life. Not surprisingly, these authors added an index to their little book which contains a list of all the clichés they have mentioned and discussed – naturally in alphabetical order.

An important aspect of this reified nature of clichés is the fact that they tend to remain unaltered over a time-span of sometimes several generations. The clichés of our speech are linguistic fossils, passed on from generation to generation, transcending as it were the many historical changes of meanings and values. Proverbs are a very good example. They remind one of mythological structures which defy all changes of meaning and values, and thus seem to laugh history in the face. Indeed, in clichés time has been frozen. Human expressions in language and behaviour tend to be in a state of flux, changing their content and form with the development of socio-cultural life. But when these expressions turn into clichés, time freezes. This is why it is so hard to change the cliché: like a magic formula it is unalterable.

If modernization is a process in which meanings and values shift rapidly and continuously, thus failing to provide the modern individual with a stable symbolic reality, clichés may come to the rescue, presenting modern man with linguistic and behavioural beacons stale and worn-out as they are in terms of semantic power. Moreover, if modernization does not only bring about rapid and continuous social and cultural changes (which, needless to add, should not be viewed automatically as social and cultural renewal), but also generates reification on a large scale, as Marxists and non-Marxists alike claim, clichés may well present the ideal moulds for modern man's consciousness. (These issues will be dealt with in a later stage of our argument.)

8 Because of this reified nature and because of their repetitiveness, clichés have the tendency to acquire a momentum of their own i.e. to become relatively autonomous *vis-à-vis* the individual in society. Without changing much in content and form, clichés are handed over from generation to generation, while the individual adjusts to them by learning to use them in daily social life. An important part of socialization consists of the teaching and learning of clichés and their appropriate emotional reflexes. The core of this learning

process is, of course, the acquisition of one's mother tongue. By learning the native language, we begin to mould our thoughts, emotions, volitions and acts according to the clichés of former generations. In this autonomy *vis-à-vis* the individual, the clichés resemble institutions. Following Emile Durkheim, we may view institutions as collective and traditional forms of thinking, feeling, and acting, providing the individual with stability and society with a durability which transcends individual human beings. The coercive moral force of these institutions prevents man and society from the threat of anomie. Following Arnold Gehlen, we may also assign to institutions the power to stimulate behaviour – something man needs badly, since he lacks the appropriate instinctive equipment by means of which the animal can survive in nature. However, ever since Marx we also know that the institutions of an historically specific society (Marx's capitalist, bourgeois society) are very much able to stifle human freedom and creativity, growing ever more strongly into meaningless and alienating fetters, which tend to severely limit the vitalistic forces of production. It is not necessary to be a Marxist to realize that fully modernized societies are indeed in danger of erecting an 'iron cage' (Weber) in which human life itself tends to become a cliché.

As will become increasingly clear during the course of this argument, clichés resemble institutions in all this very much. In fact, we could view clichés as micro-institutions, while the institutions of modernized society tend to grow into macro-clichés.

9 Finally, we should realize that because of their autonomous nature clichés may eventually attract a new meaning which differs from the original meaning that had gradually grown stale from overuse. In fact, clichés may lose their original semantic strength and pith, and their functionality may supersede their heuristic relevance, yet they will not be devoid of all contents of meaning.[10] When a waitress cleans our table, gives us the menu, and says 'How are you today?', she is, of course, not really interested in how we happen to fare this very day; it is a professional signal which does not require a precise answer. In this sense meaning has been superseded by function. Yet, the phrase does carry a meaning, and a very functional one at that: it indicates that the waitress is ready to serve us. As this point clearly demonstrates, we will now have to define the concepts of meaning and function more precisely, and discuss their relationship in more detail.

Meaning and function

The central argument in the previous section was that the original

17

meaning of a cliché – its semantic power or heuristic pith – has gradually been superseded by its functionality due to its repetitive overuse. If someone uses the cliché 'sadder but wiser', nobody will ask him to explain with more semantic precision why and how he has become sad, what kind of sadness he is suffering from, and what exactly the nature of his acquired wisdom is. When a speaker at a political rally uses terms like 'democracy' and 'freedom' over and over again, nobody present will ask him to explain their precise meaning. They have no precise meaning anymore, but they are employed to create a mood, to mould a mentality, to prepare a behavioural attitude. Likewise, when in a sermon the preacher constantly speaks of 'Jesus, our Lord' and 'Jesus, our Saviour', he uses semantically empty words which should create a religious mood. There is a very appropriate religious cliché for this: 'to open one's heart'.

These examples, which the reader can easily multiply himself, indicate what is meant by the supersedure of meaning by function. Which functions clichés can carry on in society will be discussed in more detail in chapter 3. At this point we must first further clarify the concepts of meaning and function.

Throughout this study, we will struggle with the fact that clichés are wellnigh unavoidable; even a critical treatise of the cliché, like the present one, is bound to fall prey to them. However, a conscious attempt can be made to use clichés critically – to clarify them as much as possible within the frame of reference of the whole argument. One of the most inflated concepts in philosophy and the social sciences is without doubt 'meaning'. It usually connotes a lot, but if one searches for the precise meaning in which an author employs it, one usually remains in the dark. Indeed, such concepts as meaning, function, structure and culture carry all the characteristics of clichés.

In this study the concept of meaning, as the related concept of function, is used in a specific way and in order to avoid any undesirable vagueness, I shall first give a terse definition and then further comment on it. Those familiar with his brand of social psychology will notice that I have been inspired mainly by Mead's explanation of meaning as an emergent property of social interactions:

Meaning is that quality in human interactions which enables
a participant, as well as an observer, to not only cognitively
and emotively follow the interaction and participate in it,
but to also predict and understand the next few stages of the
further development of the interaction.

As is well known, to Mead the mechanism of taking the role (or attitude) of the other is essential and instrumental to the emergence of meaning in interaction. In my definition I add the time dimension of anticipation which I shall call prolepsis.

The following example clarifies the definition. When a teacher in the social interaction of teaching and learning explains a theory, and when questions arise during the course of his explanation which warrant the answer 'wait, I come to that in a moment', he knows that his explanation of the theory in question has made sense to his students, that he was understood, that his words were meaningful. That is, the students were not only able to follow the teacher (cognitively, perhaps also with empathy), but while taking over and internalizing his role or attitude as teacher and addressing themselves internally as if they were their own teachers (Mead's 'taking the role/attitude of the other'), the students were apparently able to think a few steps ahead. They could, as it were, anticipate or predict the next few stages of the teacher's explanation with relative ease. They were also able to anticipate the semantic content of the further explanation – not to its very end perhaps, but at least a few steps further.

In the ancient art of rhetoric, *prolepsis* stood for the anticipation of possible objections to a speech. This anticipation enabled the speaker to provide answers to objections before anyone had the chance to even raise them. In other words, the speaker takes the role/attitude of the listener while preparing or delivering his speech, and he tries to assess in advance what possible objections could be raised.

I should like to change the meaning of the concept prolepsis slightly and to apply it to Mead's theory of interaction. Prolepsis is the capacity to anticipate the next few steps or stages in a social interaction. If it occurs – as in those questions of students to which the teacher must answer 'wait a moment, I come to that in a moment' – one can be assured as partner in the interaction that meaning has indeed emerged. A student in our example of teaching–learning would have been unable to ask any questions or raise any objections, if he had lagged behind cognitively and experienced great difficulties in following the speaker's arguments. Or, if one wants to object successfully (i.e. to stand a good chance of winning the ensuing argument) to a speech or part of it, one must not only internalize the role/attitude of the speaker but also try to think ahead, to engage in prolepsis. As a result, speakers who wish to forestall such objections often try to confuse their audiences by setting up a verbal smoke-screen which does prevent any kind of prolepsis. When the students of our example lag too far behind for too long, they will no longer be able to concentrate, i.e. to internalize the role/attitude of the teacher and to follow the course of his argument attentively. This is called appropriately 'losing one's audience'. The interaction might still continue, but it will be mechanical, without internalization and prolepsis. That is, the interaction has lost its meaning and continues for sheer functional reasons – for instance, because the teacher has to fill up the teaching hour of the schedule. This is the crucial difference between symbolic interaction and behaviouristic exchange; needless to say clichés prosper in the latter instance more than in the former.

There is a distinct sequence in internalization and prolepsis, the former being a precondition for the latter. Mead's 'taking the role/ attitude of the other' is an *a priori* for all social interaction (an *a priori*, incidentally, which we also find in Simmel, when he tries to give an answer to the question of how society is possible). It is through this mechanism of role/attitude-internalization that meaning emerges out of an exchange of gestures, giving rise to meaningful, symbolic interactions. Only within these meaningful interactions can human beings engage in prolepsis. In short, internalization is the *a priori* mechanism which causes the emergence of meaning, while meaning is that quality in an interaction which enables its participants to engage in prolepsis. Thus, whenever one observes prolepsis (as in the case of those questions which called for the response 'wait, that will be explained instantly'), one can be assured that the interaction in question is more than a behaviouristic stimulus–response exchange, namely that it is a meaningful, symbolic interaction.

The preceding definition and discussion of the concept of meaning indicates already how the concept of function can and will be defined:

> Function is that quality in human interaction which enables
> an actor to realize a certain course of action, according to
> the stimulus received from an interaction partner, and inde-
> pendent of any cognitive and emotive internalization of roles
> or attitudes on the part of the actor.

This aspect of social interaction has been sharply and adequately formulated by the traditional, behaviouristic stimulus–response scheme. To take up our example once more, in the process of teaching and learning, internalization and prolepsis are not always indispens-able. In primary school, for instance, children are well-nigh be-haviouristically trained in the basic rules of arithmetic. They learn how to multiply, add, divide and subtract, and they are not supposed to ask such questions – philosophically highly relevant and mean-ingful – as why $2 + 2 = 4$, or why $2 - 2 = 0$. In order to realize the educational goal – i.e. the ability of students to fully master the basic rules of arithmetic, without which they could not function well in society – the teacher has ruthlessly to brush aside such questions relating to the meaning of arithmetical rules. Similarly, while teaching how to read, he should not get involved in any discussion on the meaning of words, and the possible relationship between words and reality.

In order to acquire these skills, students have naturally to use their brains (their IQ – if such a 'thing' exists at all). But they do not need to internalize the role/attitude of the teacher in a proleptic thrust, since they do not have to ponder over meanings. Multiplication tables have to be learned by heart behaviouristically and they are to be exercised in a very repetitive manner. This is learning not by 'taking the role/attitude of the other' but by repetition and reinforcement mechanisms (Skinner). After the rules of arithmetic have been learnt mechanically – by sheer repetitiveness – they can be applied without the interference of reflection. When one pays a bill, one does not ask why two times two should be four. One has mastered the basic rules of arithmetic, and triggered as here by a bill, these rules stand ready for use, without the intervention of reflection; there is no need for internalization and prolepsis. Behaviour occurs in an efficient and functional sequence of stimulus and response, while meaning is superseded by function. It is only when we begin to ask philosophical (and admittedly very complex) questions as to the nature and foundations of mathematics, that function will be superseded by meaning again.

Until now we have discussed meaning and function separately. We must now discuss their mutual relationship. To begin with, it stands to reason to view both meaning and function as two inseparable aspects of human behaviour. A 'symbolic interactionist' approach that neglects the mechanistic stimulus–response dimension of interactions is as theoretically inadequate as a 'behaviouristic' approach that neglects the symbolic dimensions of internalization and prolepsis. Both approaches are mutually complementary and their customary separation in the modern social sciences – usually defended on methodological and erroneous ontological grounds – is actually totally uncalled for.

As is usually the case with sectarian disputes, the ongoing debate between the adherents of the two approaches has not made much progress. In sociology, for instance, arguments are still in use which were applied in the ill-fated exchange between McIver and Lundberg, back in the 1930s. Two erroneous arguments have in particular haunted this dispute: on the one side, prime *methodological* emphasis is placed on natural science as *the* model for all the sciences, while on the other side prime *ontological* emphasis is placed on the supposedly 'essential' difference between meaningless nature (to be studied by the natural sciences) and meaningful, human culture (to be studied by the humanities).

This is, of course, not the place to discuss the much neglected solution of Heinrich Rickert, namely to *methodologically* distinguish between two mutually complementary scientific approaches, namely de-historicizing ('generalizing') *Naturwissenschaft* and historicizing ('individualizing') *Kulturwissenschaft*. These are not mutually separable disciplines, but two approaches, two methods, two perspectives on reality, being the two poles of a continuum between which the various scientific disciplines are located. It should be noted that Rickert – and he was followed in this by Max Weber – did not propose this division of scientific labour because he divided reality ontologically into 'nature' and 'culture', as Dilthey had done prior to him (*'Natur'* and *'Geist'*), and as McIver still did in his debate with Lundberg. He came to this two-fold distinction of the sciences for *epistemological* reasons (human knowledge, within and outside of science, moves always between the poles of generalization and individualization) and for *practical-methodological* reasons (an established discipline like history has necessarily developed methods which differ markedly from the established natural sciences – what then is this difference?).

Within the social sciences, the behaviouristic approach is the legitimate representative of *Naturwissenschaft*, while the symbolic-interactionist, interpretive approach represents *Kulturwissenschaft*. A conflict between the two can only emerge when one either absolutizes the natural-scientific methodology, or engages in ontological reifications of 'nature' and 'culture'. Both errors can be avoided relatively easily within the context of Rickert's methodology.[11]

A completely different and, in my opinion, more interesting and important problem is the question of whether there are specific historical and socio-cultural conditions which foster either the supersedure of meaning by function, or the supersedure of function by meaning. This, of course, is a sociological question. It can be dealt with most lucidly by taking the relationship between *religion* and *magic* as example.

Meaning is definitely superseded by function in a socio-cultural context which is dominated by magic. Having learnt magical skills and/or having a consciousness which is predominantly moulded by magical forms of cognition and emotion, one is able to behave like an automaton i.e. mechanically, without internalization and prolepsis. Magical behaviour – if taken idealtypically – is programmed behaviour, not least because it is believed that magical power, *mana*, resides in repetitiveness. As much as religion has historically been penetrated by magic, it differs – if taken idealtypically – from magic significantly in that it tends to ask questions which are related to meaning. Unlike magic, religion requires believers to understand and accept certain theoretical tenets, certain doctrines about man and the world; it requires believers to identify with fellow believers in a community. Not least does it require believers to identify with the religious leaders who have founded their power and authority on the mechanisms of internalization and prolepsis on the part of the members of the religious community. In magic the world is viewed in a deterministic way: human beings, animals, objects and events run their predetermined, causal courses. It is an enchanted world ruled by blind but deterministic forces. In religion, on the contrary, certainly if it is dominated by what Weber has called 'a prophetic ethos', the world is viewed in terms of moral human responsibility: human actions evolve from motives and are directed towards other human beings – they are meaningful, social interactions for which the actors are accountable. Moreover, religious reality is not characterized by repetitiveness but, as prophetic religions in particular have demonstrated, by history. This historical reality is viewed as an understandable, meaningful reality. It is thus within religion that world-views could be developed which tried to explain reality in a systematic manner – from mythology to theology and philosophy. It is in religion that behaviour became organized in a rational manner (cf. the church). It is in religion that behaviour became subjected to a rational ethos which regulated conduct in everyday life (cf. protestant ethic). In contrast, magic does not develop a meaningful world-view; rather it contains techniques to wield power over reality. Magic does not organize believers into larger organizations that promise to provide religious redemption. At most it develops guild-like groupings of magical professionals. Magic does not know an ethos which spells out the rules of responsible conduct.

From this idealtypical juxtaposition which, of course, hardly ever occurred in such a sharp way in historical reality, Weber drew the conclusion that magic could not contribute to the rationalization of the Western world – a process which he consequently labelled 'the disenchantment of the world'. It was religion, more specifically the prophetic religion of redemption, and still more specifically Calvinist puritanism, which in its radically anti-magical thrust welded the forms of modern rationality. In Calvinism we witness the supersedure of magic by religion which in the history of human civilization had only once before occurred in such a dramatic fashion – during the time of the prophets of ancient Judaism. Apart from these two socio-cultural contexts, religion has always been superseded by magic. Only with the emergence of modernity did magic encounter its truly fatal adversary: modern science.

Weber tended to view religion and magic in terms respectively of rationality and non-rationality or anti-rationality. Consequently, he viewed the process of modern rationalization as a disenchantment, as a decline of magic. It seems to me that religion and magic should rather be viewed in terms of two different kinds of rationality.

23

Ironically, Weber has himself formulated these two types: religion represents value-rationality (his *Wertrationalität*), whereas magic represents goal-rationality (his *Zweckrationalität*), and not rationality and non-rationality or anti-rationality. Mannheim successfully renamed these types of rationality when he spoke of *substantial* and *functional* rationality.[12]

When an individual is substantially rational he is able to see and understand meaningful relations and structures in reality. To him, reality does not constitute chaos and meaningless anarchy, but he discovers and understands structures, relationships and combinations which are not obvious on first sight. When an individual is functionally rational, he is able to set a certain goal and then to design consciously certain means which can adequately realize this very goal. Magic is in this sense functionally rational: in order to get rain, the sorcerer believing in the power of his imitative magic, sprinkles water and recites formulas. Religion, in contrast, is substantially rational: man and the world are viewed and interpreted in terms of meanings and of moral categories. The universe is viewed as an ordered whole, a structured *Gestalt*, in which even the forces of darkness and destruction receive their proper place (theodicy).[13] Thus, when religion or, for that matter, modern science, triumphs over magic, it should be viewed as a supersedure of functional by substantial rationality, of function by meaning – and not of non-rationality by rationality. Likewise, when we speak of meaning and function in the context of social interaction, one should not define meaning as a non-rational or even irrational, and function as a rational quality in interaction. Both are rational: meaning tends to be substantially rational (*wertrational*) and function tends to be functionally rational (*zweckrational*). Thus, when we define clichés in terms of a supersedure of meaning by function, this does not at all mean a supersedure of the non-rational in speech and behaviour by the rational. The cliché rather presents a switch from substantive to functional rationality. It is a switch from 'symbolic interactionist' internalization and prolepsis to 'behaviouristic' repetitiveness and reinforcement.

Conclusion

The main sociological observation of this chapter has been that a cliché should be seen as a specimen of human expression which has lost much of its original ingenuity and semantic power, but gained in social functionality. Or, in other words, clichés are the result of an inflation of meaning – they can be likened to the many coins of an inflated economy. Moreover, we view this yielding of semantic power and heuristic pith to social functionality not merely as an increase in rationality, but rather as a transition from substantial to functional rationality – a supersedure of meaning by function.

Up till now two questions have yet remained unanswered. First, are there specific historical and socio-cultural conditions which enhance the supersedure of meaning by function and thus the distribution and use of clichés? I have said briefly that two such conditions can indeed be mentioned: societies where magic predominates and societies that have fully modernized. We shall limit our further discussion to the latter and only refer to the former by way of comparison. I shall try to demonstrate in the next chapter that modernity is very much the result of a supersedure of meaning by function and that this inevitably has led to the emergence of what I call a 'clichégenic society'.

The second question relates to the very functionality of clichés. If they can indeed be characterized by the supersedure of meaning by function, of substantial by functional rationality, what then are their functions in daily social life? The following two chapters will address themselves to these two questions.

2 The clichégenic society
The elective affinity between modernity and clichés

Introduction

Some Russians are increasingly apprehensive these days about the invasion of foreign, mainly Anglo-American, words into their language. Words like 'service', 'outsider', 'hobby', and 'office' are transliterated in the Cyrillic alphabet and look like *servis*, *autsaider*, *khobby* and *offis*. One linguistic purist, a high ranking official at the newspaper of the Soviet Communist Youth League, has recently voiced his protest and wrote: 'We simply do not have the right to leave after us a thin, clichéd and faceless language, for this is unjust for the following generations.'[1] Since modernization has progressed the farthest in the USA, American English and much of its *slang*[2] has become the *lingua franca* of modernity. Thus, wherever a nation modernizes on the scale of North-America (which is called significantly, though falsely, 'Americanization'), hackneyed American words like 'jeans', 'sneakers', 'hamburgers', 'disc-jockeys', and the all-American 'hi' as a means of greeting, are liable to penetrate into the native language, just as American-based multi-nationals are liable to sneak well-nigh invisibly into the native economic system. The quoted Russian purist was on his guard: 'I am against this mindless borrowing of foreign words, many of which not only do not spiritually enrich us, but soil our native speech, depriving it of purity and internal strength.'[3]

In the present chapter I shall argue that modern society fosters the use of clichés in language and behaviour to such an extent that clichés become tyrannical. In other words, in a fully modernized society clichés are hard to avoid; they tend to become the moulds of consciousness, while their functionality penetrates deeply into the fabric of socio-cultural and political life. It is in this sense that I use the neologism 'clichégenic society' – modernity generates and, fosters clichés. This concept needs some further introductory clarification.

I shall view the relationship between clichés and modernity in Weberian terms of elective affinity (*Wahlverwandtschaft*) and not of a mono-causal, deterministic influence of the latter on the former. Apart from the fact that such a mono-causal argument easily tends to forget that clichés have indeed tyrannically ruled over societies that were not yet modernized (cf. the rule of magic in pre-modern societies, or medieval scholasticism in the ban of Aristotelean philosophy, or seventeenth—century court life ruled dictatorially by *etiquette*), it precludes the possibility of viewing the relationship between modernity and clichés in terms of mutual influence. Both modernity and clichés have their historical origins and autonomous developments, but the nature of modernity is such that it strongly fosters the functionality of clichés. The other way about, clichés are moulds of language and behaviour, moulds of consciousness and awareness that do fit modernity perfectly well. They present modernity with a human consciousness that supports and even further stimulates modernization. Or, to formulate it differently, clichés are moulds of speech and behaviour which are very appropriate and functional to the speech, feeling, thought and action of truly modern human beings. They thus enhance the modern characteristics of contemporary society. Through clichés, modernity can be more readily expressed in speech, in cognitive knowledge, in emotions and in actions, just as, according to Max Weber, the mentality of the Calvinist puritan fostered the 'spirit' of capitalism. In short, clichés are the appropriate moulds of modern consciousness and the very corner stones of modernity. This will be the main theme of the following pages.

Modernization and the decline of aura

In his well-known essay on 'The Work of Art in the Age of Mechanical Reproduction', Walter Benjamin developed a theory concerning the effects of industrialization on art. His argument can be generalized and applied to our present discussion on modernization and clichés. Most germane to the problem of clichés and their functionality in modern society is, I think, Benjamin's notion of the decline of aura during the process of modernization.

The objects we perceive, Benjamin says in his essay, whether we call them 'natural' or 'cultural', appear to us as *unique* objects which we experience from a distance. When we see, on a sunny afternoon, 'a mountain range on the horizon', or 'a branch which casts its shadow over you'[4], we experience them as unique objects – we cannot reproduce them, nor can we ever duplicate this experience of them, while we also experience them from a distance – we cannot carry them with us, preserving them in order to have them always near us and at hand. Benjamin proposes to call this combination of *uniqueness* and *distance* the aura of objects perceived and experienced. He believes that the truly great works of art are always characterized by such an aura.

To this he adds the dimension of *permanence*. The aura of perceived and experienced objects links them to the past, casts them in a tradition, renders them durable. Experiencing the aura of a great painting in a museum enables us to view its beauty as something which transcends the here-and-now. The aura of the paintings of such masters as Vermeer, Rembrandt and Van Gogh has obviously transcended the many profound socio-cultural and political changes and revolutions of Western society, and it is quite likely that Picasso's *Guernica* will still strike its viewers long after we have died. It is the aura that renders such eminent works of art permanent. Incidently, Benjamin also stressed the more superficial dimension of this permanence: the physical conditions of these paintings have changed (they suffered damages and were restored), their owners have changed (they have been sold and bought by individuals or museums), thus they have a history of their own.

In sum, uniqueness and distance constitute the aura of a work of art and a crucial characteristic of this aura is the time-transcending permanence. It is interesting to observe, I should like to add, how this very aura may arouse aggression. In 1975 the famous *Nightwatch* by Rembrandt in the Rijksmuseum, Amsterdam, was suddenly attacked by a man with a knife, who turned out to be mentally deranged and later committed suicide. It took several months to restore the damage which from now on remains part of this painting's history, like a scar on a person's face.

In the 1960s a Dutch artist, whose own artistic products have demonstrated very little aura to date, proposed literally to throw all the Rembrandts, Vermeers, Ruysdaels, Van Goghs and what have you on the refuse dump, since the bourgeois veneration extended to them was clearly symptomatic of undemocratic authoritarianism. (Aura, as we will see presently, is indeed a kind of authority.) A small band of like-minded colleagues of his, occupied somewhat later the huge exhibition hall of the Rijksmuseum in which the *Night Watch* hangs, threatening to throw red paint at it, unless some of their socio-political demands, the substance of which is irrelevant here, were met.

Benjamin argues that mechanical reproduction – the procedure by which objects of art can be massively reproduced and sold – destroys the three dimensions of aura. A reproduction of a painting by, for example, Van Gogh is no longer unique but, on the contrary' massively available. It also lacks distance since we can easily buy it, carry it home, frame it and hang it on the wall of the living room. Finally, there is no permanence either: we very easily dispose of the reproduction when we have grown tired of it. In sum, the difference between a real Van Gogh and a reproduction lies precisely in the presence and absence of aura. Works of art without aura, I should like to add, are without exception very boring.

Benjamin has emphasized the objective nature of this aura. Using permanence as an example, he warns against viewing it as something static but, on the contrary, this permanence is 'something thoroughly alive and extremely changeable'. Yet, it does transcend the point of view of a historically specific generation. That is, it does possess objectivity:[5]

An ancient statue of Venus, for example, stood in a different traditional context with the Greeks, who made it an object of veneration, than with the clerics of the Middle Ages, who viewed it as an ominous idol. Both of them, however, were equally confronted with its uniqueness, that is, its aura.

The objectivity of aura is also demonstrated by the fact that truly great works of art possess *authority* and *authenticity*. It commands, we may add, a viewer to look at a work of art, to hold his breath, to either adore and admire or abhor it. That is, if a work of art has aura it 'does something' to those who perceive and observe it. It is not just a passive object exhibited in a museum, but it is as much an active subject which is commanding[6] and works on its observers. According to Benjamin, this aura of art is doomed to decline with the rise of modernity, in particular with the rise of technology and the increase of mass production. The masses of modern society want to possess objects in great quantities for easy and instant consumption. This entails a distinct decline of uniqueness and distance. The commodities of mass society are massively reproduced, massively consumed and very easily disposed of, or exchanged. Benjamin refers to[7]

the desire of contemporary masses to bring things 'closer' spatially and humanly, which is just as ardent as their bent toward overcoming the uniqueness of every reality by accepting its reproduction. Every day the urge grows stronger to get hold of an object at very close range by way of its likeness, its reproduction. Unmistakably, reproduction as offered by picture magazines and newsreels differs from the image seen by the unarmed eye. Uniqueness and permanence are as closely linked in the latter as are transitoriness and reproducibility in the former. To pry an object from its shell, to destroy its aura, is the mark of a perception whose 'sense of the universal equality of things' has increased to such a degree that it extracts it even from a unique object by means of reproduction.

This is, of course, not the place to discuss critically Benjamin's theory of aura and of its decline in the modern age of reproduction. The theory applies very much to reproductions of paintings, and also perhaps to recordings of music. It is, however, very questionable if it could be applied, as easily as he does, to the cinema. Even in Benjamin's days, prior to the Second World War, films were more than reproductions of reality; in many cases, films are true works of art with their very own aura.

This is also not the place to ask to what extent Benjamin's notion of distance has been influenced by Bertolt Brecht's theory of *Verfremdung* (i.e. creating a distance between actors and audience during a performance by all sorts of alienating techniques).[8] Like Brecht, Benjamin claimed to have been heavily influenced by Marxist theory and he saw Marx as his intellectual and political ancestor. However, in many respects he resembles much more the kind of cultural observer De Tocqueville and Weber have been, than revolutionary critics like Marx, Engels and Lenin.

Instead of engaging in such a critical discussion of Benjamin, I prefer to apply his concept of aura and his theory of aura's decline during the rise of modern society, to our present discussion of the clichégenic nature of this society. However, before we do so, I must briefly compare the concept of aura with Weber's 'notion of charisma' and 'the routinization of charisma'.

Since 'charisma' has gradually become a sociological cliché, it has lost much of its original semantic power and heuristic pith. However, if we compare it to such a relatively unknown concept as that of aura, it may regain some fresh meaning. An important difference between both concepts lies in the fact that Benjamin applied aura primarily to the perception and experience of objects, while Weber viewed charisma much more broadly as a social force which comes to sociological light in a specific type of authority and leadership. The similarity lies in the notion of extraordinary uniqueness: the daily routine is, as it were, broken and people are inspired to act and feel in a manner which differs from the patterns to which they have become accustomed. The aura of a work of art and the charisma of a person or movement arouse also a sense of beauty and duty simultaneously. That is, they are commanding and convincing, and they provide a sense of meaningfulness which is easily corroded by the routines of daily existence. In sum, both aura and charisma transcend function and bring about the experience of meaning.

A third similarity lies in the notion that both aura and charisma are bound to decline when a society begins to modernize. Although Weber believed that all charisma, independent of the historical variable of modernity, is doomed to eventually routinize, he was also convinced that modernization, and in particular bureaucratization, could eventually bring about routinization to a degree that has rarely been realized in the history of mankind. Thus, just as Benjamin saw a decline of artistic aura in 'the age of mechanical reproduction', Weber saw a decline of authoritative charisma in 'the age of rational bureaucracy'.[9]

The decline of aura and the rise of the cliché

Benjamin himself generalized his notion of aura beyond the realm of art and claimed in particular that the decline of aura should be seen as the *differentia specifica* of modern society. In order to elaborate this point, I take an example from a sector of modern daily life which is far removed from the realm of aesthetics. The example is admittedly pedestrian but the reader should keep two things in mind: first, cultural sociology and cultural analysis focus on meanings and values and their changes not just in the rather obvious sectors of the arts, religion, law, science and other parts of a so-called 'super-structure', but as much on the daily affairs of mundane and pedestrian life; second, the functionality of clichés, so closely tied to the decline of aura in modern life, is not at all an exalted affair but affects us unobtrusively in the routines of daily life. Indeed, most clichés function in a pedestrian way which is precisely the reason why it is so hard to observe and analyse them. The example then is the buying and selling of groceries in a typically modern set-up, set against the same exchange in a typically pre-modern context.

Compared to the keeper of a little grocery shop in a yet pre-modern and rural society, who not only sells his merchandise but also discusses with his customers the weather, the latest bits of gossip and the affairs of village politics, the personnel of a modern supermarket engage in remarkably little social interaction with customers. In fact, in a supermarket we actually do not need speech at all: we select our merchandise, pay at a counter manned by a silent cashier performing highly automated and routinized movements, and we leave without an exchange of greetings. In this transaction (because that is still what it is) there is no permanence, no uniqueness and no distance involved at all. This becomes particularly clear if we compare it to the same exchange in the pre-modern grocery shop. The shopkeeper is known by name and his customers know his family history, perhaps even going back a few generations.

31

Yet, despite this familiarity, characteristic of 'mechanical solidarity' (Durkheim), the shopkeeper knows his social place in the informally guarded and traditionally grounded hierarchy of status and power. In other words, there is uniqueness and distance, founded on the permanence of tradition. This has all changed fundamentally in the supermarket. The customer does not know and does not even care to know the personnel of the supermarket by name or family background. In fact, selecting his merchandise the customer hardly notices the personnel, unless he needs some assistance which usually consists of a brief, functional exchange. As a result, he does not at all care to place them in a hierarchy of status and power: to him the personnel are social 'non-persons'. In this respect the supermarket does not have any hierarchy but is as 'democratic' as a graveyard. Permanence is also totally absent: the supermarket does not have any history related to the history of the social community. Nobody cares to know who founded it, who the actual owner(s) is (are), or what precisely the chain is to which it belongs. The supermarket, of course, is much more functional than the little village grocery shop but it is also a socially 'dead' place. People behave like automatons, and their behaviour is a prime example of the supersedure of meaning by function.

(Perhaps I should at this point state emphatically that these observations – somewhat stretched, of course, for the sake of the argument – do not represent any positive or negative value-judgement on my part. If the reader would insist on knowing my evaluation of the supermarket compared to the pre-modern grocery shop (although the reader should not be interested in such a triviality as the author's shopping preferences), I must admit that I intensely dislike the alleged cosiness of such little shops for various reasons. For one, the gossip by pre-modern shopkeepers and their customers can be extremely vicious, its effects of social control very tyrannical and stifling. Moreover, being used to efficiency and functionality in modern society, the inefficiency of such shops can be charming for the duration of a vacation, but usually turns out to be rather frustrating after a few weeks. In sum, normatively speaking, I do believe that the decline of aura in modernization has been accompanied by an increase in efficiency and freedom. However, this normative belief of mine is irrelevant to the present discussion. Moreover, this discussion is interested only in the rise of the cliché which is believed to be tied to the decline of aura.)

Until now we discussed only the decline of aura in the interaction of buying and selling. But the merchandise itself, bought and sold, also exhibits this growing lack of aura. In a supermarket the products of mass consumption are displayed in a very functional manner (pre-modern grocery shops are in comparison often 'crummy' and sometimes simply dirty): uniformly wrapped (no uniqueness), to be selected and picked up by the customer (no distance), and without any history or tradition (no traditional recipe, just nutritional and commercial functionality).

Food, in particular, has lost its aura in the age of the supermarket. A rather extreme example is the so-called 'TV dinner' which totally lacks the flavour of a carefully prepared meal. In this respect, much of the stock of frozen food may be mentioned as well: it is very functional but totally lacking in aura.[10] The same applies in the world of fashion to 'blue jeans'. Originally (during the 1960s) denim symbolized the values of what was called the 'counter culture'. It allegedly crossed the boundaries of class, sex, generation and culture. But nowadays the blue jean is nothing but a functional piece of clothing – indeed the cliché of modern fashion.[11]

There are, of course, some sociologically interesting counter-movements. The increase in the number of small *boutiques* in our metropoles is an example. A boutique can restore some degree of aura in the interaction between buyer and seller, and it can focus on a relatively small stock of goods, maintaining some degree of uniqueness, distance and permanence. The question is, however, how economically viable such independent and small enterprises can be in the long run.

As to the decline of aura in modern food, the little shops selling macro-biotic food definitely represent a kind of counter-movement. Likewise, small and exquisite restaurants, boasting the charismatic art of their cook, may be viewed as attempts to restore aura. However, as of yet, such counter-movements are but small phenomena on the fringe of modern society's mass consumption.

We could add more examples, focusing on the various sectors of today's culture. Take, for instance, the world of so-called 'classical music'. We hardly realize nowadays that not very long ago music lovers could only hear their favourite symphony or opera a few times in their life, particularly if such favoured music did not belong to the standard repertoire of performing artists – a symphony by Bruckner, or an opera by Janacek. In order to hear such a piece of music, one had to be constantly on the watch for a rare performance. Going to hear it then must have been an exhilirating experience (uniqueness), which would easily be related in memory to earlier, rare performances (permanence). Moreover, the only way to really get to know this music i.e. to master it mentally, was to buy the score (quite often a piano transcript), and to play bits and pieces at the piano (distance). Today, the music lover has a choice of recorded performances. He can carry them home, and listen to them passively as often as he wishes. He can even buy tapes, and play them while he drives. As a result of this abundance, there is a real danger of

33

saturation as with someone who has eaten too often of the same exquisite dish. Moreover, when he then goes to a concert and hears a live performance, he will probably pay more attention to the mode of performance – the technique and style of the interpretation – than to the actual content of the composition. That is, the music has lost its surprises, only the performance may still come as a surprise – although even that is rarely the case these days. Not surprisingly, this remarkable shift in attention from composition to performance has been discovered quite some time ago by the record companies: the covers of their records announce the name of the performer – a famous conductor, a famous violinist or pianist – in huge letters with the name of the composer somewhere in a corner.

This shift of emphasis from composition to performance has had its influence on the art of performing itself. Not rarely 'star' soloists want us to believe that, if there is any aura in the music they perform, it is brought about by their particular interpretation. The result is a growing subjectivism and expressionism in performances of 'classical music'. The soloist imposes his emotions on the composition, using the latter as a means to express himself. Consequently, his record company will announce on the cover of his recordings that his performances are 'authoritative' and 'authentic' – not the composition. Arturo Benedetti Michelangeli, a contemporary pianist who has consciously isolated himself from the modern, commercialized routine of the performing arts, said recently in a rare interview:[12]

> The pianist should not express *himself*. The principal thing – the most essential thing is to enter the spirit of the composer. It is what I tried to instill in all pianists who have come to study with me. The trouble with today's younger pianists is their fixation on their own personality. This is a pitfall and it will lead them nowhere. What's important is to abandon oneself to the thoughts and ideas of the man who conceived the music. To learn the literature is only the beginning. A pianist's true personality will emerge only when he has made contact with the composer. Only when the composer possesses the pianist, can one think about making music.

In sum, we buy and consume goods – material as well as immaterial – in great quantities in modern society. The production of these goods takes place with their functionality in view: they should sell well and be easily, readily and in massive quantities consumable. Should such mass-produced goods still possess some degree of aura, we are liable to consume them so intensively and repetitively that we eventually become saturated. We then grow tired of them, they begin to bore us and consequently we dispose of them. The *disposal of objects* is then another remarkable feature of modernity which deserves some attention here. It has been discussed extensively in the recent avalanche of debate on pollution, but it has rarely been viewed in terms of the decline of aura and the supersedure of meaning by function.

Let us take furniture as an example. In pre-modern society, furniture would often last for several generations, thus becoming part of the material history of a family. Today furniture is usually made to last no longer than a decade. If it has not broken by then, we grow tired of it and want to dispose of it. Naturally, advertising tries strongly to stimulate this attitude. Like other modern goods for consumption, furniture thus tends to lack aura. The chairs we sit on, the table we eat at, no longer belong to a family history and when they were bought, they were most likely not selected for their unique style. They were also not made by hand but mass-produced in factories – easily bought and just as easily disposed of.

The consumer counter-movement is in this case observable in the growing popularity of *antiques*. In fact, the purchase of expensive antiques may well be interpreted as an attempt on the part of modern man to buy aura. Meanwhile, this attempt is rarely successful, because if one possesses only a few antique pieces, these are too much set apart from the rest of the furniture; if there are, however, too many antique pieces, the room changes into a kind of museum. In both cases, aura is not restored at all.

Very much related to this is the *disposal of human beings* in modern society. I am not just referring to the obvious examples of genocide during and after the Second World War, but would rather focus here on some elements which are less obviously woven into the fabric of modern society.

Modern man, to take a first example, seems to dispose of a friend or a spouse with relative ease because relationships like friendship and marriage are no longer primarily founded on a sense of mutual responsibility, guarded by traditional values and norms. Instead, these relationships are primarily based on the desire to consume emotions instantaneously and continuously. They, therefore, bear very little aura and are doomed sooner or later to reach a point of saturation. The friend or spouse is then disposed of, and exchanged for the next one. Loyalty is almost as old fashioned a virtue nowadays as honour!

A second example presents the institutionalized disposal of two categories of human beings who apparently are no longer functional within modern society: the aged and the insane. In many pre-modern societies, the elderly in the community possessed authority and wielded some kind of power because it was believed that their many years of age had provided them with an inimitable wisdom. The

35

mentally deranged were not infrequently believed to possess some kind of divine charisma, indispensable to the functioning of society. But with the rise of functional rationality in the process of modernization, the aged and the insane became increasingly useless. They were, therefore, disposed of into old people's homes and asylums.

Finally, do I stretch the argument too far, if I extend it to the issue of abortion? Does not the modern attitude towards abortion (which has recently become very explicit in the debates on legalization) indicate that the unborn child is no longer viewed and experienced in terms of uniqueness, distance and permanence?

There definitely is an elective affinity between the decline of aura and the clichés. In fact, the nature of clichés could easily be described in terms of decline of aura. As we saw in chapter 1, clichés are very much the result of reproduction. It is primarily the repetitive use of words, thoughts, emotions and acts which turn these expressions of man into clichés. We have then described the nature of these clichés in terms of the supersedure of meaning by function, of substantial rationality by functional rationality. This supersedure can also be described in terms of a decline of permanence, distance and uniqueness.

It is, of course, obvious that a cliché is devoid of any uniqueness. Repetitiveness is the core of its nature. However, clichés do exhibit a certain degree of permanence. They are, as we have seen, traditional casts of language and behaviour which are passed on from generation to generation. But this is not at all the permanence Benjamin referred to when he described the phenomenon of aura. The permanence of aura, as Benjamin saw it, resembles much more Bergson's *durée* – that meaningful, uninterrupted sequence of subjectively experienced time, attentively followed by consciousness. Clichés, on the contrary, are reified chunks of stale experience in which time has been frozen. When somebody speaks, one cannot quantitatively measure the amount of thought and emotion that he expresses. It is, however, quite possible to count the number of clichés that roll off his tongue; they can be singled out from the speaker's stream of consciousness and set apart. This certainly is not what Benjamin meant by aura's permanence.

Finally, clichés cannot be characterized in terms of distance either. They are easily and readily available. In using them we do not have to stop and think, we do not have to invest much psychic and mental energy. Having been fully socialized in a particular society, the clichés of this society will lie in store in man's consciousness, ever ready ready to be triggered and used. The conclusion seems to be justified – the functionality of clichés will increase when aura begins to decline. However, even apart from the decline of aura, modern society can be interpreted as a historically specific configuration that strongly fosters the rise of the cliché. This will be argued in further detail in the next section.

The clichégenic conditions of modern society

While pre-modern societies are usually characterized by various socio-cultural layers or buffers between the individual and society-at-large (notably, the family, the community, and religious organizations), the individual in modern society is more or less directly exposed to the social and political structures of modern society. In his work, in his leisure activities, and even increasingly in the privacy of his nuclear family (by the incursion and necessity of dealing with licenses, insurances, taxes, welfare, etc.) the modern individual constantly runs into the bureaucratic mechanisms of various socio-cultural organizations and into the particularly well developed bureaucracies of the welfare state. If he is to function properly at all (i.e. efficiently), the modern individual must be able to mould his behaviour according to pre-determined roles, learned during a long process of socialization. It is very hard for the traditional intermediate structures, such as the family, the community and the church, which formerly were the main providers and defenders of meaning and thus occupied central positions in the social structure at large, to provide these modern roles with any viable content of meaning. They have been driven into the corners of the modern social structure, yielding their power and influence (in particular in matters of meaning) to science and politics. Likewise, their influence in matters of economic and social order has been taken over by the state bureaucracy and the super-organization of large corporations which quite often extend their power far beyond their national borders as well as beyond the limits of the economic sector. But neither science and politics, nor the state bureaucracy and the corporations are able to provide the individual with meaning; rather they demand his ever lasting functionality. In this situation, it seems to me, clichés are very useful: they are the 'appropriate' moulds of consciousness!

The notion that the modern individual is directly exposed to the influence of modern social and political structures (so-called 'mass-society model'), is usually and justifiably criticized by referring to the *voluntary associations*, ranging from social clubs to professional unions. However, in view of the presently discussed supersedure of meaning by function, one should keep in mind the following facts: first, most voluntary associations are strongly linked to modern, abstract society by their inevitable bureaucratization; second, many of them are also tied to the welfare state by legal regulations and subsidies; third, the members are only partially committed to their voluntary associations, entertaining often loyalties to several of them, not rarely in a sequence of time. As a result modern voluntary associations can hardly assume the functions of conveying and defending meaning in the same way as this was done by the pre-modern intermediary structures such as the family, the church and the community. They might provide the individual with some meaning, but this meaning is as partial as the one provided by the modern community, church and family. Therefore, it is in terms of the sociology of knowledge that I maintain that the modern individual is directly exposed to the social and political structures of his society.

In a pre-modern setting the individual was, of course, also required to adhere to rather formal patterns of behaviour, perhaps even more strongly controlled and more severely enforced than is the case in modern society. However, unless totally immersed in the mechanics of magic, these patterns of behaviour were *meaningfully grounded* in a basically *religious tradition*, and within this traditional context borne by the family, the community and the religious organization. Sure enough, the tradition entailed a very heavy burden and had its share of formalism, but if at all reflected upon (which in fact would rarely happen), this burden could always be explained in terms that made sense to the individual. Moreover, pre-modern societies knew ritualized revolts against tradition – from ceremonial clowns breaking taboos in a ritual performance to carnival festivals in which the members of traditional society could engage in various licentious and anarchistic activities.[13] But after having observed and experienced chaos and anarchy for the duration of such ritualized festivals and performances, one was glad to return to the routine of daily life and assume the burden of tradition again. In other words, ritualized anarchy had a heuristic function and was far removed from modern anomie: it demonstrated to man that he could indeed forsake tradition and deliver himself to his instincts and to the vitalistic forces of chaos, reducing himself to an animal. But, having seen and experienced it, the individual was happy to resume the chores of tradition in an everyday life routine again. The only thing in modern society that comes close to such a 'ritualized' interruption of daily routine, is the yearly vacation. Modern individuals go through a great deal of trouble in order to leave their home and work for a few weeks. They are usually quite happy to return and not rarely this return is the greatest pleasure of the whole vacation. The 'ritualization' of these vacations, how-ever, is of course of a commercial, not of a religious and thus meaning–spending nature.

In sum, the patterns of modern behaviour are predominantly social roles which are adhered to for functional–rational reasons and are experienced as components of abstract, yet near (i.e. not mediated) structures. There is neither permanence nor distance, nor are these roles to be played in a unique manner: whether one lives in Europe or the USA, the roles demanded by modern abstract society are very much the same.

Modern society is a society without tradition. That is, the past is not experienced as a meaningful component of the present. As a result, modern consciousness has increasingly grown a-historical and functional. This is demonstrated by various forms of pragmatism and functionalism. Even attempts to restore a sense of historicity are generally evidence of the modern *'post-histoire'* (Gehlen). They usually do not at all restore tradition but tend to romanticize the past in a nostalgic manner. More than anything else, *romantic nostalgia* – which is, of course, at least a century old – emphasizes once more the a-historical consciousness of modern man. A society firmly rooted in a meaningful tradition does not know a *temps perdu* for which it restlessly and nostalgically searches. The indeed widely spread, pre-modern myth of a paradise lost was never a nostalgic dream, certainly not when it occurred in a setting in which magic was superseded by religion: the prophetic religion of ancient Judaism and Calvinist Puritanism. Here future-oriented eschatology precluded both a-historical, magical fixation and romantic nostalgia for a lost past.

It has been said many times in sociology that due to an intensive division of labour, much needed in order to realize an increased production which was made possible in turn by modern science and technology, modern society has developed into a *pluralistic society*. By this concept we usually mean the notion that the individual is required to play many different roles which together do not constitute a coherent identity. The pre-modern individual learnt during his socialization – which often came to a definite end with the rites of puberty (unlike in modern society) – a traditionally grounded and coherent set of behaviour patterns (Durkheim and Gehlen's 'institutions'). These patterns were more or less predestined for him before birth and did indeed constitute a coherent identity which was very closely tied to the 'collective consciousness' (Durkheim) of his society. The modern individual, in contrast, continues to learn and unlearn various roles which in fact incorporate different, autonomous identities with different, sometimes conflicting values and norms. (Even the roles of male and female, which were thought to be biologically fixed, now can be and are being changed.) In a modern setting, a young man can be exposed at once to the demands of his family, the office, the university and the army, each of them imposing on him identities and related moral demands which do not cohere at all and even, in some cases, may severely conflict.

39

Thus, he must be able to change roles and identities like jackets, giving rise to the experience of a distance between his Self and the surrounding social structures. In his famous essay on the web of group affiliations, Simmel has already noted that the modern individual, because he is a kind of intersection of different groups, tends to experience societal structures as autonomous realities – autonomous, that is, *vis-à-vis* himself as well as mutually autonomous. At the same time, he will experience himself increasingly as an autonomous subject without existential ties to the surrounding societal structures – the very origin of modern subjectivism and individualism. Autonomization of society is thus paired with the autonomization of the individual, and there is, of course, no point in asking which caused which, both are functions of the process of modernization.[14]

We encounter here, in terms of Benjamin's concept of distance, an interesting and significant state of affairs. As we have seen previously, the modern individual is directly exposed to society and to the state. He experiences social and political structures, particularly in their bureaucratic functionality, constantly and without intermediary structures that could convey meaning. As a result, he will experience them as 'objective', 'repressive', 'abstract', 'alienating' structures – that is, if he were at all to become conscious of his situation as in a kind of sociological awareness. Most of this experience, however, will be pre-reflective, and that only enhances the supersedure of meaning by function: abstract society is by and large a society in which substantial rationality has increasingly been superseded by functional rationality. This is, of course, a clichégenic condition.

(We should distinguish clearly between two rather different kinds of distance. There is, first of all, the *sociological distance* in terms of the discussed intermediary structures between the individual and his surrounding social and political structures. In the process of modernization, I argued, this distance has declined, exposing the individual more or less directly to various, often contradictory demands of commitment and loyalty. Durkheim called this *anomie*. This should, however, be distinguished from the *socio-psychological distance* in terms of the awareness of (often pre-reflective) experience of meaninglessness i.e. of not being able to relate meaningfully to the surrounding (sociologically rather close) social and political structures. Following Marx, this distance can be called *alienation*. Various 'classical' sociologists have argued – albeit in different terminologies – that during modernization sociological distance gradually decreased, while socio-psychological distance increased. Or, to formulate this tersely: anomie and alienation are functions of modernization.)

The clichégenic nature of this autonomization of the modern

individual *vis-à-vis* his surrounding social and political structures can be further substantiated by focusing on *the free-floating nature of the values, meanings, motives and norms of modern society*. That is, not that the intelligentsia is socially free-floating, as Mannheim believed, but the values, meanings, norms, the related ideas, notions, theories and ideologies of modern man in general are, so to speak, up in the social air. William Isaac Thomas summed it up cogently, when he said of modern society: 'There are rival definitions of the situation, and none of them is binding.'[15] This, I shall now argue, is another very strongly clichégenic condition.

Because of the decline of sociological distance and the increase of socio-psychological distance, the modern individual tends to continuously ask questions where the pre-modern individual would have taken things for granted. Following Arnold Gehlen, the German sociologist Helmuth Schelsky once called this state of affairs rather aptly, modern man's *Dauerreflexion* (permanent reflection). Hence, when the individual is no longer able to relate to traditional institutions in a taken-for-granted manner, as is the case in modern society, he will constantly raise questions and reflect upon meanings, values and motives: 'Why do I do this, and why do I do this the way I do it?' In fact, he broods (sometimes explicitly, as in existentialist philosophy, usually implicitly, as in a kind of continuous relativism) over the meaningfulness and legitimacy of the institutions of his societal and cultural surroundings. He tends to search for answers outside the alleged 'objectivity' of the institutions – in the often irrational abodes of his subjective, cognitive and emotive life. In this anti-institutional subjectivism, many modern individuals claim to be searching for 'authenticity' and they do so by endless reflections and discussions. Existentialism provided them with the appropriate philosophical ideology.

It should be noted first, that this anti-institutional subjectivism in no way impedes modern social and political structures from functioning. On the contrary, since modern abstract society is characterized by the supersedure of meaning by function, subjectivism supports functioning, since it weakens the formerly strong ties between meaning and tradition and thus robs meaning of its stable ground. To give just one example, the often emotional and irrational revolts against 'the Establishment' during the 1960s in no way impeded the functioning of abstract society. On the contrary, the anti-institutional subjectivism inherent in all types of protest in the 1960s[16] strongly supported the further supersedure of meaning by function, because it delivered meaning to the highly unstable and vicarious abodes of inner, emotional life where it easily evaporated into all sorts of contradictory irrationalities. Threads of existentialist philosophy were mixed with fashionable theorems drawn from psycho-analysis, depth-psychology and Marxism, often garnished with rather vague allusions to Zen Buddhism and Hinduism. Meaning should have superseded function, but the consequence (we may assume, unintended) of it all was that meaning became stranded in irrationalities and snobbish fads, while function could be carried on by the abstract structures of social, economic, cultural and political organizations. In short, subjectivism supports abstract society in that it severs meaning from traditional institutions while delivering it to the irrational abodes of emotional life. This only supports the supersedure of meaning by function.

Meanwhile, since meanings are no longer traditionally attached to institutions but have become reflection material – to be experienced emotionally and to be discussed and reflected upon endlessly – they have become gratuitous and quite arbitrary. This is also the case with the values, norms and motives of modern man. They are, to cite Thomas once more, incorporated in rival definitions of the situation, none of which are morally binding. They have lost stable ground. They float around in thin social air, ready to be picked up and to be disposed of again.

In such a situation where meanings, values, norms and motives are no longer tied to traditional and institutionalized responsibilities, but float around 'freely' as if in a kind of vague and gratuitous morality, marriage is bound to lose its original institutionalized status within the social structure. It will most likely continue to exist as an institution (it has, after all, a very basic societal function), but the related meanings, values, norms and motives detach themselves from the traditional institutional ground, and are incorporated in a vague and morally gratuitous ideology of romantic love. Such traditional values as 'marital loyalty' and 'parental responsibility' will be conspicuously absent in this ideology, because they are generally not emotionally gratifying. The nuclear family will most likely continue as an institution in abstract society (it too has a probably indispensable societal function) – shrunk into a small unit of consumption. But the familial meanings, values, norms and motives will leave this institutional base and spread over abstract society as a vague, morally gratuitous ideology of familism, distributed mainly, though not exclusively, by the many women's monthly journals. Likewise, the church will continue to exist as an institution albeit in a corner of the modern social structure. But outside this institutional home base, a vague religiosity will spread over society, penetrating into other institutional sectors in a free-floating, uncommitted, gratuitous manner. Its leading position in the social structure might well have been taken over by the modern state. But also in this case we can observe the same process. The state is viewed and experienced as an alienating Leviathan to which it is hard to relate in a participatory manner. Yet, everybody is being told these days that he should get politically involved, and in the mass media (especially on television) politics has become a kind of gratuitous entertainment, nice to look at but morally not binding at all. Only when things get out-of-hand too obviously as in the last stages of the Vietnam War, will people mobilize successfully. However, in the context of the present discussion, it is not the political success of this protest which should attract our attention, but the feelings of solidarity and purpose that were aroused in these years which seem to be significant: beyond the vague and irrational phraseologies of different ideologies, people met and protested against a blatant injustice. Obviously it was a very rare experience, and after the war was over, everybody returned to abstract society and its free-floating values, norms, meanings and motives.

The universities offer a last example. They are gradually reduced in scope and quality by all sorts of measures and reforms, but they are most probably here to stay as institutions of the abstract society. Meanwhile, in this case also, a vague ideology spreads beyond its institutional home-base into society. Nowadays, everybody teaches everybody and there is continuous talk of 'permanent education', as if life is not worth living without at least a bachelor's degree. Not surprisingly, subjectivistic, anti-institutional fantasies arise about education-without-discipline (Summerhill) or education-without-schools ('deschooling society'). It is typical of our age: science-without-universities, religion-without-churches, medicare-without-hospitals, performing arts-without-theatres or concert halls – all of them floating 'freely', 'creatively', liberated from tradition and traditional bonds. The individual is promised that thus he will discover his 'real' Self. But what such gnostic ideologies really promise, are swimming-pools-without-water.

Many examples could be given here. I restrict myself to just one instance in which the combination of religiosity and familism gives a strikingly clear picture of free-floating, gratuitous, and morally totally unbinding meanings, values, norms and motives.

In September 1977[17] *Ladies' Home Journal* published an interview with a famous American show-business star. I quote from this interview extensively:[18]

> She talked about religion, something that became important to her three years ago. She was raised a Christian Scientist, but then, when she started doing Yoga exercises to heal an injured neck, she responded emotionally to meditation. She began to read philosophy. 'I think we are all a reflection of God', she said, 'and that people have their individual personalities, but that the closer you get to the centre, the

more you find that everybody is a reflection of one mind or being.' What she has tried to learn from this, she said in complete seriousness is: 'I try not to be phony. To me that means treating people well.' She talks a lot about what she calls 'good values' and 'morality' and there is probably, beneath the Hollywood veneer, the large house, the pool table and the tennis court, some strait-laced sense of morality. Family life, for example, is very important to her. She and her husband, J.H., producer of the show, are home from work every day by five. She often drives her three young daughters to school herself and shops with them for things like skateboards and birds. Through the years, her husband's eight children by his first marriage have all lived with them, but now they are grown up and away.

The typically modern vagueness of meaning can be found to an enormous extent in the social sciences and the humanities. The reader can almost at random take any contemporary treatise in ethnomethodology or phenomenology to corroborate this point. Arnold Gehlen used to call this modern man's '*Schwungradvorstellungen*' (trapeze-notions).

Criticizing Harold Bloom's theory of 'misreading poetry', Hilton Kramer recently made the following significant remark:[19] 'It leaves him so much room for self-contradiction – for saying one thing and meaning both it and something else or perhaps nothing at all – that it would be incautious of us, not to say naive, to jump to obvious conclusions.' It is an excellent description of the state of consciousness that I try to analyse here.

Since they are no longer tied to a traditional institution or institutional sector, these free-floating values, norms, meanings and motives lack any permanence. They are as easily embraced, as rejected again. As organizers of ideological organizations· and movements very well know, it is extremely hard to bind individuals to a cause for a long period of time. In other words, their participation is not so much based on loyalty to a cause, as inspired by the typically modern desire to consume certain values, meanings, norms and motives for a while. These are just fashionable for the moment – widely commercialized because of their potential profit (sold to the public as 'best sellers' or 'top hits'). They are as easily and suddenly dropped again and exchanged for other values, norms, meanings and motives. In other words, they are the emotional and intellectual toys of modern man and there is no permanence in his playing with them.

Since these values have to satisfy irrational and emotional demands, they are not characterized by distance. When adopting an ideology, modern man often identifies with it totally and intensively, until he becomes saturated and discards it. However, before saturation point has been reached, he is not able to treat the ideology – its free-floating meanings, norms, values and motives – 'objectively' and *par distance*. (Much of the protest against so-called 'value-freedom' in the social sciences can be interpreted in these terms!) After the saturation point has been reached, the heroes of the ideology are soon forgotten. Who speaks of Bishop Robinson these days, or who remembers the writings of Herbert Marcuse? The ideas of the former were attractive since they could be indulged in without any binding commitment to a church, the theories of the latter were passionately and rather uncritically accepted since they too could be espoused without any binding commitment to a political party. Their ideas were declared to be unique and of lasting relevance, in particular by those who used them with a profit motive (their publishers and the leaders of action groups). But if looked at from some distance, this claim could, already in the days of their first appearance, be dismissed. Robinson simply popularized some basic theorems of Barth (one of the last great system-builders in theology) and of Bonhoeffer, reducing both of them to the level of manipulable clichés; Marcuse did something similar. He constructed theoretical collages – at times, admittedly, very good ones – out of the works of Hegel, Marx and Freud.

At this point, the reader will certainly raise the question how this state of affairs can possibly be viewed as a clichégenic condition. In fact, one could argue that modern subjectivism and its anti-institutionalism (in which individuals consume virtually at random free-floating values, norms, meanings and motives), constitutes a state of affairs in which clichés – those mini-institutions, those rather rigid and reified chunks of past experiences – cannot and will not function at all. This argument, however, only seems plausible if one looks at the relationship between clichés and modernity superficially. And here we have arrived at the heart of the matter.

As I stated earlier, it would be highly fallacious to claim that modern, abstract society more than any other societal configuration in the history of human civilization creates, fosters and maintains a tyrannical functionality of clichés. Medieval culture, to take just one example, had its share of clichés (cf. scholasticism under the yoke of Aristotelean clichés), while all cultures in which religion remained superseded by magic, were caught by cliché formalism. However, unless religion was totally wiped out by magic, this pre-modern formalism was still couched in an institutional tradition which provided individuals with a sense of meaningfulness and above all with a stable, because collective, consciousness and identity. To formulate it briefly, function remained tied to meaning,

45

while meaning remained tied to tradition which was incorporated in the institutions. Again, only in a society in which religion (i.e. that component in a culture which provides man with meaningful interpretations of the universe and of history) is totally superseded, or even stronger: brushed aside by magic (i.e. that component in a culture that provides man with techniques by which he can manipulate spiritual powers), will cliché formalism reign tyrannically. In such a society – which can probably only be conceived ideal-typically – function would reign rampantly. It is safe to state that in most pre-modern societies function remained tied to meaning, while meaning remained tied to tradition through the institutions. Clichés did exist in these pre-modern societies but their functionality was contained by the power of institutional tradition.

This, however, changed drastically in the process of modernization. Industrialization, urbanization, the dramatic rise of science and technology, bureaucratization, and the capitalist mode of production (or its various socialist variants) were, of course, unable to wipe out meaning – just as magic never did so in pre-modern society – but they certainly brought about the previously discussed supersedure of meaning by function. It should be added now that these very same processes, collectively called 'modernization', increasingly severed the bonds between meaning and traditional institutions. That is, the quality of our interactions that enable us to understand these interactions, to relate to them cognitively and emotionally, and even to anticipate their further course of events – i.e. the quality that enables us to communicate in a sensible manner – has lost much of its stable ground, has become gratuitous and spurious. Many of our interactions run through their rather pre-determined functional course. As to meaning, we moderns are very much 'up in the air': there are many meanings in modern society, and none of them is binding. Together with values, norms and motives, these meanings constitute a vast sea of cognitive vagueness, emotional instability, and moral uncertainty.

It is my contention that *clichés* function as beacons in this vagueness, instability and uncertainty. They are points of recognition, things to get a hold on, stable points to relate to. While norms and values, meanings and motives are no longer firmly tied to traditional institutions, but float around as vague ideologies and hazy philosophies, being consumed gratuitously in subjectivist reflections and emotions, clichés will gain in importance as fixed points of orientation without – and this is of immense importance – demanding of the individual who uses the clichés, that he return to traditional institutions. In short, in the cognitive vagueness, emotional instability and moral uncertainty, brought about by modernization, clichés provide the individual with clarity, stability and certainty

They are, of course, very artificial, if seen in the light of traditional institutions, but that is still better than having no clarity, stability or certainty at all.

This argument leads to an important conclusion. When under the impact of modernization a society grows abstract – which means basically that the cognitive and emotive bonds between the individual and the traditional institutions grow thin and ephemeral, rendering meanings, values, norms and motives free-floating – *clichés* will have the tendency to function as *substitutes for institutions*. They will, so to say, fill up the institutional void. Clichés are, of course, particularly equipped to perform this function. As we have seen in chapter 1, clichés resemble the institutions very much. In fact, we have called them mini-institutions and argued that in some historical instances institutions seem to become macro-clichés. We can now, however, point at the essential difference between clichés and institutions: the latter have their ground in tradition which is able to prevent the rise of cognitive vagueness, emotional instability and moral uncertainty; the former have their ground primarily in their functionality (to be discussed further in chapter 3), making for *artificial* clarity, stability and certainty. Yet, as was said, this is still better than no clarity, stability and certainty at all!

There is still another reason why clichés fit modernity so well. As reified chunks of past experiences they can easily be picked up, but since they lack any traditional ties, they can as easily be disposed of. In other words, they do not require any long-term commitment and loyalty, nor do they demand any moral responsibility. Thus, they do present beacons in the vast sea of free-floating values, norms, meanings and motives, yet they do not tie the individual to any traditional-institutional commitment, loyalty and responsibility.

Finally, as we have seen clichés manage to trigger speech and behaviour, while they avoid any reflective pondering of meaning. Also in this respect clichés are able to function as substitutes for institutions in a situation in which the bonds between the modern individual and traditional institutions have weakened. Man needs the institutional stimulation of behaviour in order to survive in nature, because he lacks an adequately co-ordinated and equipped set of instincts. Institutions, as Gehlen has argued successfully, are in a sense man's substitutes for the lack of instincts. When, however, these institutions lose their hold over man, as has happened in the process of modernization, man has no instincts to fall back upon for his behavioural stimulation and ends up in a rather dangerous subjectivism in which he searches for emotional 'shocks' and 'kicks'. Gehlen believed that this has indeed happened in modernity and that, in terms of evolution, modern society therefore constitutes a kind of 'dead-end street' – he called it '*Spätkultur*'.[20] I should like to argue, however, that institutions have not completely lost their grip over modern man but that rather they have been compartmentalized in relatively autonomous sectors with a limited realm of influence over individuals, while in addition the clichés have taken over much of the functions of the institutions, as it were in the interstitial voids between the compartmentalized sectors. Granted that this substitution of clichés for institutions is rather artificial and totally lacking in the long-term stability of tradition, it still is more than no stability at all.

It should be noted that the clichés also come in rather handy in the permanent reflection of modern man. Schelsky originally asked the question of how this *Dauerreflexion* could be institutionalized and thus stabilized at all.[21] The answer must be, I am afraid, that this kind of subjectivism cannot be institutionalized. It can, however, be relatively and necessarily temporarily stabilized by clichés.[22] Clichés provide meanings, however stale and worn-out these may be, and simultaneously manage to avoid any further reflection of meaning, thus halting the permanent reflection for a while.

The most 'gratifying' and 'satisfying' clichés in the 1950s have been obviously coined and distributed by existentialists: the 'jargon of authenticity', as Theodor Adorno named it aptly.[23] In the 1960s Marxism provided once again the 'indispensable' clichés: the jargon of alienation and liberation, of infra- and super-structure. Freudianism, sometimes mixed with existentialism and Marxism, as in a neo-hellenistic syncretism, has produced the jargon of cultural repression. Often people joined in groups in which they would discuss, interpret, explain, defend and endlessly repeat to each other as well as to outsiders the very same clichés to which they had committed themselves for the time being. Such clichés are like mantras providing modern man with a semi-magical sense of security and stability, and in which permanent reflection can come to a temporary rest.

At this point in my argument I should like to draw special attention to the *moral dimension* of this whole state of affairs. When values, norms, meanings and motives are no longer rooted in traditional institutions but float around freely, providing material for gratuitous reflections, people will talk at length but their speech is no longer morally tied to behaviour. As a result, both speech and behaviour will become unpredictable and unreliable. Modern man is talkative precisely because he does not have to invest much cognitive and emotive energy in his speech: virtually unhampered by tradition, he can relate almost at random to those norms, values, motives and meanings to which he responsds emotionally. The free-floating ideology of his choice-for-the-moment supplies him with clichés which can be readily applied in daily speech and behaviour without really meaning much. The result is that words, thoughts, emotions and actions become rather unreliable and unpredictable. A person can say one thing, but the next moment do something quite different. This could be observed, to give just one example, among faculty members and students in the days of university unrest: a person would say one thing in private, but would speak and behave quite differently the next day in a public meeting in which everybody was bombarded by certain political clichés. This person would not consciously lie or cheat, but his words would no longer be tied firmly to his behaviour. They were instead losely tied to ideological commitments and their related clichés – commitments which could easily, well-nigh unconsciously and certainly pre-reflectively, be switched in a changed situation. This has nothing to do with situational ethics; rather it is a culturally conditioned and instilled immoralism.[24]

One interesting result of the free-floating nature of modern values, norms, meanings and motives is the fact that certain coalitions between ideological positions become suddenly possible, which in pre-modern days would have been unheard of. Roman Catholicism and Marxism, for example, have always been irreconcilable foes – politically as well as ideologically; this seems no longer to be the case. The recent political *entente* between the Vatican and the Kremlin can still be interpreted as traditional, Machiavellian *Realpolitik* on the part of these partners who, incidentally, both did not hesitate to make political deals with the Hitler regime for similar political, no less immoral reasons. Rather I should like to focus our attention on the phenomenon whereby modern priests seem to be able to reconcile their Catholic faith with certain basic tenets of Marxist doctrine, while increasing numbers of Marxists seem equally to be able to link their Marxism with certain basic tenets of Catholic doctrine.[25] For instance, referring to Marxist atheism, the Brasilian Roman Catholic priest Francisco Lage Persoa wrote in an article, published in 1968:[26]

> One could ask, at the risk of scandalizing both sides: may not that atheism be the unconscious search for the ultimate consequence of redemption? That which would signify 'finding God in the heart of man' (Paul VI), 'where, if He is not present, He will not be anywhere' (*Galileo* from Brecht).

In short, in modern life very strange chemical interactions between ideologies and world-views are possible, and we shall witness many more confusing and at first disturbing mixtures of values and motives, meanings and norms which were traditionally fixed but which increasingly loosen their institutional ties in abstract society.

Until now we have discussed the clichégenic conditions of modern society in terms of the sociology of knowledge alone. In conclusion of this section I should like to discuss a final clichégenic feature which lies more 'superficially' on the level of organizational sociology.

When social and political structures grow ever more autonomous *vis-à-vis* the individual, and when the latter experiences a socio-psychological distance between himself and these structures, society – as we have argued constantly – tends to become ever more abstract and formalistic. Not only the state, but also the various sectors of society show the tendency to emphasize means above ends, functions above meanings, forms above substance, procedures above substantive problems, functional rationality above substantial rationality. In this formalism, bureaucracy occupies an almost archetypal position, particularly in its most recent, fully automated appearance. Here human behaviour seems to be totally encapsulated by functionality and its concomitant form of rationality – what we call, often in a derogatory tone, 'red tape'.

This fully automated bureaucracy has a much neglected moral dimension: once a human error has been fed into the computer, it becomes very hard to take it out again. In due time, nobody but the computer is blamed for it. As a result, nobody can be held accountable, and thus nobody can be taken to task for the error. It is a kind of delegation of responsibility from the social realm to a machine: The *Montreal Star*, 15 August 1977 gave a very good example of this delegation of responsibility to the machine. It reported how a Dallas construction worker, who had planned to take a job with a firm in Chicago, was haunted by such a computer error for which nobody would take responsibility, absurd as the results of this were in actual fact. Two days before his departure, namely, this man received a letter from Chicago stating that his contract had been cancelled because he failed the physical examination. The letter referred to the R-3 clause which, however, related to pregnancy. He took up the phone and wanted to tell the lady of the personnel office in Chicago about this rather obvious error. After having consulted his file, she told him to call the industrial health clinic where he underwent his physical. The lady in that office checked again his file and returned to the phone to tell him that he definitely had a R-3 rating and that this was all she could tell him over the phone. The man then flew to Chicago but was told by the personnel office that rules were rules and that he had to wait for the clinic to admit to the error. But at the clinic they would just check the computer and repeat the R-3 rating. Said the plagued construction worker: 'All they talked about was the R-3 rating. No one seemed to want to translate it as meaning that a 24-year-old man was pregnant.' Indeed, in the mind of the bureaucrats concerned, meaning had been totally superseded by function: the computer had to run its course, even if the results were obviously absurd and bizarre.

Finally, a doctor at the clinic discovered that the file of a woman with an almost identical name had been sent to the personnel office of the construction firm. It took three weeks to straighten the error out. Then the man got the job. 'But', concludes the clipping, 'his new job contract has a clause that forbids maternity benefits in his health insurance for the next nine months.'

Once programmed, the computer runs its predetermined course – the modern variant of predestination. But as much as it may frustrate us, we do realize that a Luddite attack on the computer would not solve any problems. Nor is there a point of return to more traditionally anchored modes of organization. Bureaucratically organized life is necessarily and inescapably translated into shorthand codes which are *en masse* and virtually eternally reproducible. They are, moreover, reproducible without the interference of human cognition, emotion and action. To this state of affairs, clichés have obviously a strong elective affinity, while also, and conversely, computerized bureaucracy will strongly foster the cliché as the form of consciousness appropriate to its own functionality.

Conclusion

I defined clichés in chapter 1 as forms of human expression in speech and behaviour which, mainly because of their overuse and consequent repetitiveness, have lost their original ingenuity and semantic power, but maintained and in some historical cases (magic, modernity) gained in functionality. That is, clichés are not relevant for what they express (they no longer say what they originally said), but they are relevant for what they do in society: they exert social and political functions which will be discussed in more detail in the next chapter. I summarized this by the formula 'supersedure of meaning by function'.

In this chapter I have argued that clichés as moulds of speech and behaviour do fit modernity perfectly well. Clichés have occurred, of course, prior to modernization and when, in a pre-modern society magic superseded religion, clichés generally had a tyrannical influence. I have argued that clichés constitute too a perfect cast of consciousness for modernity. In this sense, clichés exert a causal influence on modernity – very much like the alleged influence of the 'puritan ethos' on the capitalist mentality (*'Geist'*). But one should also argue the other way about. Modernity very strongly fosters the formation and use of clichés in speech and behaviour – like the alleged influence of the capitalist economy on the 'puritan ethos' which under this influence secularized into an irreligious business mentality. Thus, the neologism 'clichégenic society' should be seen in terms of Weber's 'elective affinity' clichés and modernity: mutually attract and stimulate each other.

The crucial link between clichés and modernity, enabling the elective affinity between them to occur, consists of the discussed supersedure of meaning by function. This supersedure did, of course, also occur prior to modernization but it was only in our fully industrialized, bureaucratized and technological society that this supersedure became an all-pervasive and thus sociologically essential phenomenon – comparable historically only to those societies which had been subjected to a strong supersedure of religion by magic. This pervasive supersedure of meaning by function is the heart of the rationalization process which Weber called, rather erroneously, 'the disenchantment of the world' (literally: the de-magicizing of reality!). In clichés, as we have seen, meaning has also been superseded by function.

As a further sociological dimension I have added the Benjamin theorem of the decline of aura during the process of modernization, and linked it to Weber's theorem of the routinization of charisma; both are relevant to a sociological understanding of the position occupied by clichés in modern society. I then set out to discuss more specifically the clichégenic conditions of modern abstract society. For the sake of clarity, I shall now summarize these conditions:

1 During the process of modernization, the traditional intermediary structures between the individual and his surrounding social and political structures – i.e. the family, the community, the church, various voluntary associations – whose function it was to convey and defend meanings, as well as values, norms and motives, have been gradually pushed into the corners of the social structure at large, making room for science, technology and politics, and for the large economic corporations. Since these can hardly assume the meaning-conveying and defending function of the traditional intermediary structures, the individual is, in terms of the sociology of knowledge, directly exposed to his social and political structures which impose functional role demands on him. As to the meanings, values, norms and motives, the void left by the traditional intermediary structures is easily filled up with clichés.

2 Because of this very pluralism, the individual in modern society will increasingly experience social and political structures as autonomous, 'objective' structures *vis-à-vis* himself as an equally autonomous person with a 'subjective', potentially independent life.[27]

One important result of this double autonomization is the fact that values, norms, meanings and motives, which in pre-modern society were always closely tied to traditional institutions, begin to loosen their institutional ties and to float around socially 'free' and morally gratuitous. That is, rather than incorporating the moral bonds of tradition which demand loyalty, responsibility and thus accountability, these values, norms, meanings and motives become material for permanent reflection and endless discussion. The criteria of their validity are no longer rooted in tradition, but have been diverted in a subjectivistic manner to emotion and emotional gratification. This very subjectivism and anti-institutionalism, however, has strongly fostered the functioning of abstract society and in particular the whole development towards the supersedure of meaning by function. In fact, it has produced and distributed many of the clichés of modern man (cf. existentialism, psycho-analysis, depth-psychology, Marxism).

3   This free-floating nature of modern values, norms, meanings and motives causes a very fundamental cognitive vagueness, emotional instability and moral uncertainty. In this situation clichés can come to the rescue. They provide clarity, stability and certainty as fixed points of recognition, as things to get a hold on, as stable points to relate to – albeit this clarity, stability, and certainty remain rather artificial if compared to the clarity, stability and certainty that traditional institutions could offer pre-modern man.

4   In this situation words and deeds are no longer tied to each other. A person may one moment say one thing, and the next moment do something totally different. This very much constitutes a clichégenic condition, since clichés are moulds of consciousness in which the original content of meaning has lost its relevance and has been superseded by sheer functionality. Now, when words are no longer morally tied to deeds, and when deeds are consequently no longer understandable and morally accountable in terms of certain words, clichés form the ideal cast of mind and mentality: to begin with, they do not really say what they say!

5   In this situation traditional institutions lose their power to stimulate speech and behaviour. Since the human individual has only few, ill-coordinated instincts to fall back on for such stimulation, he will have to search for other 'behavioural resources'. Next to all sorts of artificial, emotionally gratifying, though hardly stabilizing, 'kicks' and 'shocks' (to be discussed in a different frame of reference in chapter 4), clichés may again come to the rescue. To be sure, they do not stimulate behaviour as institutions do, but they trigger it as in a stimulus–response mechanism. Thus clichés seem to fill up the void that is left by the decline in importance of traditional institutions during the process of modernization.

6   Finally we discussed a rather obvious and notorious clichégenic condition, when we focused on the phenomenon of bureaucracy, particularly in its most recent, fully automated aspect, here the supersedure of meaning by function seems to have reached its very limits. Often the ultimate of functional rationality contains the seeds of the substantial irrational, of the absurd and the bizarre. This is among others demonstrated by errors that have been fed into the computer and consequently began to acquire a momentum of their own. In due time, nobody can be blamed and held accountable for such errors, but the computer – which is, obviously, absurd. But apart from such extreme cases, bureaucracy in modern society very much tends to demand functional speech and behaviour, and a fully functional cast of mind and mentality. It stands to reason that clichés again present the perfect moulds for such a consciousness, and thus the perfect supply to this bureaucratic demand.

We shall now turn to a more specific description and analysis of the social and political functions of clichés in modern society.

3 Clichés unbound

The social and political functions of cliches

Introduction

When meaning is superseded by function to the extent to which this is the case in modern, functionally rationalized society, the cliché becomes ubiquitous and very influential. Wherever we are, in the living room or at the office, in the lecture hall or the hospital, at a child's bed or at a deathbed, clichés are hard to resist. They are readily available and they are applied without the interference of cognitive reflections.

Indeed, when one begins to think about it, one suddenly realizes how easily clichés are exchanged, how rarely we hesitate to use them in daily life, and above all how seldom we apologize for their use. As a matter of fact, we usually accuse a person of the use of a cliché only when we quarrel with him, when we are out to score a point. The cliché formula in such a case is usually: 'Of course, we all know that, the point however is. . . .' The cliché is countered by a cliché, just as laughter can only elicit laughter as an adequate response·

The present study is primarily interested sociologically in the relationship between clichés and modernity. However, the question is legitimate, whether – independently of the historically specific clichégenic conditions of modern society – clichés do not belong to the general human condition. In other words, should clichés not be viewed also, in terms of philosophical anthropology, as indispensable components of human nature, just as the biological genes and instincts, and the cultural institutions belong to the human condition? Much like Mead's gestures, the clichés seem to lie at the threshold of the biological and the sociological. We must, however, restrict ourselves. The present discussion does not take place in the framework of philosophical anthropology and should not get involved in an ontological analysis of the clichés.

55

We must ask the sociological question as to whether there are specific historical and sociological circumstances and conditions in which the balance between meaning and function is distorted (i.e. in which the former is superseded by the latter) to such an extent that the functionality of clichés becomes tyrannical. This question runs, of course, parallel to the other sociological question, whether – given the fact that institutions are anthropologically indispensable – there are specific historical and sociological circumstances and conditions that foster anomie and alienation. Meanwhile, as was argued in the foregoing chapter, modern society can indeed be viewed sociologically as such a specific configuration: it fosters the functionality of clichés, while at the same time, clichés present the moulds or casts of consciousness which fit modernity perfectly well.

What, then, are more specifically the functions of clichés in general and in modern society in particular? We shall first discuss two functions which are general; i.e. which are not yet specific for modern society. We shall then gradually move to those functions which are typical of this society, notably those of a commercial and political nature.

Throughout the following discussion, the reader should keep in mind the two basic principles that are at work in the functionality of clichés:

a clichés manage to avoid cognitive reflection, influencing human individuals in a behaviouristic manner – i.e. they do not so much institutionally stimulate behaviour, as trigger it mechanically;

b essential to the functionality of clichés is their repetitiveness – in a behaviouristic stimulus–response process one must repeat the stimulus over and over again, until the organism has learnt to respond without the interference of reflection.

Finally, a brief explanation of the adjectives 'social' and 'political', used in the sub-title of this chapter, is needed. Both are meant here in a rather general way: the former refers to the host of daily inter-actions, thus those functions are called 'social' that assist or even enable these interactions; the latter refers to the conscious attempt and ensuing techniques to influence other people's behaviour, to exert some kind of power over them, and thus those functions are called 'political' which assist or even enable these techniques. Sometimes both adjectives will also be used in a more technical sense, referring respectively to the society (or social structure) and the polity (or the state). It will be quite clear when these adjectives are used generally, and when they are applied in the more technical sense.

Clichés as the knots of daily communication

It is quite amazing to observe how rarely people are totally silent while in each other's company. Social life seems to be an ongoing chain of interactions, very much borne by continuous speech and conversation. In Western societies we are usually silent when among strangers in public places – in a restaurant, on an escalator, in the underground; but when among acquaintances, friends, colleagues or family members, we feel almost compelled to interact and talk. Naturally, this massive amount of daily speech interaction can only be realized at all, if the bulk of it runs off automatically i.e. without much cognition and emotive effort, and with little psychic invest-ment. It is on this primary level of everyday life that clichés seem to be particularly indispensable. These 'convenient reach-me-downs' (Fowler) enable us to conduct our incessant interactions and talk without too much cognitive and emotive energy. 'How are you today?', the waitress asks while routinely placing a glass of water in front of us. 'Fine thank you', we murmur while reading the newspaper or studying the menu – and often we do not even look at her. Of course, we are not really required to answer her question and tell her how we really feel and are. The question was a professional, functional sentence and not a communicative question: it was more of a signal, or a gesture like a professionally kind smile; it requires a response in kind. That is, both the question and the response are clichés which facilitate a routine interaction without the need for any cognitive and emotive investment. Originally, the question had a meaning. The foreigner, not yet used to the routine communications of our daily social life, might still be able to experience this original meaning that for us has long since lost its semantic power and heuristic pith. He is, therefore, liable to be pleasantly touched by this kind interest in his personal well-being on the part of the waitress, and he might seriously respond to the question. That means, he is not yet acquainted with the routine of social interaction, so tersely formulated by the cliché 'keep smiling'. Soon enough, however, he will learn that the original meaning has been superseded by a professional function – this question is but a cliché which requires a cliché as response.

In order to be able to communicate efficiently in social life, we must conduct the greatest part of our social interactions as routine. Daily social life would simply be impossible if we had to ponder every single sentence and move, investing cognitive and emotive energy in every situation that occurred. Clichés are the indispensable and rather ingenious means for the realization of this social objective. They enable us to communicate without the need to reflectively internalize the attitudes of our interaction partners and to mentally and emotionally anticipate the further course of the interaction as in a proleptic thrust. In fact, clichés enable us to interact mechanically, without Mead's mechanism of 'taking the role/attitude of the other' – i.e. without mutual identification, without empathy, without reflection. By means of clichés we are able to interact and communicate smoothly, routinely and in a facile manner. It must be stated emphatically, therefore, that clichés are indispensable to social life, as indispensable, I should add, as the institutions; they are an essential contribution to the routine fabric of daily social life.

This primary social function of clichés can be further substantiated by an *e contrario* argument. Hence, an individual who wants to be original and creative in his social interactions all the time, and who therefore tries to avoid the use of clichés at all costs, is as tiresome in daily social life as a person who tries to be funny all the time. It is very hard to relate to such a person, because he will require that others also avoid the use of clichés. This puts a heavy strain on the interaction. (If one *really* wants to avoid clichés all the time and at all costs, one should retreat from social life radically, like the anchorites of old.)

Daily social life is a convention-ridden reality and this pedestrian fact constitutes the very foundation of social order. In it, we follow routine courses of action from one situation to the next: I wake up, eat breakfast, travel to work, work in the office, have lunch, attend a meeting, return home, etc. The greatest part of my social interactions and communications in these various situations are predetermined and routine, framed by sets of role behaviour which enable us to think, feel, and act efficiently and relatively effortlessly. Clichés are the core of these frames.[1] Without them, social life would indeed collapse. They provide it with an indispensable structure for without clichés, a society would deteriorate into a bizarre chaos. Alfred Schutz used to characterize the commonsense that guides us in the routine of daily social life as 'recipe knowledge', belonging to a 'stock of knowledge at hand'. Most of the recipes, we may add, are clichés.

Our daily social life can be viewed metaphorically as an ongoing process in which we continuously spin webs of affiliation towards others. However, the threads of these webs can easily wear thin and frail, particularly when they multiply and lose their meaningful coherence, as is very much the case in modern society. When this happens, we will need knots in those threads in order to be able to pick them up again whenever we want or need them. Clichés can be interpreted as such knots in the web of our communicative affiliations with others. A person who does not tolerate such knots in the threads that link us together, is a tiresome social partner who is liable to wear himself out, cognitively and emotively, as he must needs invent constantly new links with his social surroundings. The nineteenth century dandy (Jules Barbey d'Aurevilly, Beau Brummell, Charles Baudelaire) tried to live in such a way. But with all his '*épater le bourgeois*', the dandy himself eventually turned out to be a big bore and a living cliché.[2]

At this point, I should like to raise the question, whether there are any psycho-pathological clichés. As devoid of meaning as clichés usually are, they still belong to social interaction and human communication. Does the schizophrenic loneliness know the cliché? Although this is not at all my field of competence, I dare to suggest that in all its complexity schizophrenia might be partly interpreted as follows.

The schizophrenic has constructed a strictly private reality, the meanings and logic of which cannot be communicated to others and cannot be rationally or empathetically understood by others without psychiatric 'translation'. He is thus not able to engage in 'symbolic interaction', in a true communication, since this requires a mutual identification and an internalization of attitudes, as well as a communicability of meaning. Yet, his speech and behaviour is quite schematic, demonstrating a kind of reified structure. This indicates that he develops and uses his own, very private clichés – clichés that are only functional in his private reality, in the logic of his privately constructed world. In sum, the schizophrenic knows an utterly private 'meaningfulness' and 'functionality' which cannot be readily understood by 'normal' interaction partners of social life. As such he is the most radical anchorite one could possibly envisage. Quite understandably, at times he will suddenly resort to violence, because the private 'logic' does not seem to work, the private clichés do not seem to yield any results. This happens also in the non-schizophrenic social reality, when the clichés of an ideology no longer yield the emotional gratification for which the ideology had been adopted. This leads to an important conclusion: when clichés in which meaning has been superseded by function, cannot function (for whatever reason), they may trigger utterly irrational, cruel, bizarre and violent behaviour. In that case, the sequence follows a fatal route from meaning to function to terror. We shall return to this point in the next chapter.

Clichés as responses to embarrassment and precariousness

We all know that the routines of daily social life can suddenly and indeed quite regularly be interrupted and broken. Clichés, I shall argue now, are often used for the repair of such ruptures. Two of the main breaches of daily social routine are embarrassment and precariousness. We shall briefly discuss how clichés relate to both of them.

Somebody may suddenly do or say something that falls outside the daily course of events. For example, a young child may ask us in public an intimate question related to sexuality. We are taken by surprise and feel embarrassed, or at least ill-at-ease. Or, to take another example, we are at a party and someone who is generally respected, tells a very flat joke in an obvious attempt to be funny. We are taken by surprise and feel embarrassed. Or, finally, someone we hardly know suddenly confides the private secrets of his emotional life to us; we did not expect it, we do not want it, and we feel embarrassed.

In all these instances, we do not at first know how to respond adequately, what to answer, say, or do. There are, in general, two responses, two reactions that can be readily applied, without much cognitive and emotive effort: laughter and clichés. In both cases we refuse to respond seriously as in a 'symbolic interactionist' manner; we simply refuse to reflectively ponder the involved meanings, values, norms and motives.

By our laughter (often just an embarrassed giggle) we try to wave the embarrassment away, and above all to abort any further meaningful interaction. By the use of clichés we refer the embarrassment back to 'normal', social life. They are real finishers, knock-down arguments which, like laughter, prevent any further symbolic interaction – at least not in the impending, embarrassing direction. A widely used cliché in an embarrassing situation is the interjection 'incidentally'. We do not want to continue the interaction in the embarrassing way in which it is going, and we say: 'Incidentally did you know that. . . .' Or we may say: 'By the way did you realize that. . . .' In both cases, it is suggested that the interaction is not interrupted, while in reality its direction is radically changed and a totally new subject of discussion is being introduced, leading away from the embarrassment, sending the interaction back to the routines of daily social life. It is an ingenious device to restore routine communication and commonsense, with very low cognitive and emotive costs.

Situations that exhibit the precariousness of social life are infinitely harder to mend. I refer here in particular to situations which confront us with senseless suffering, as are encountered in cases of severe illness, and death. When confronted by such events, reality seems to lose its meaningful co-ordinates and it is, consequently, very hard to react and respond adequately. Once again, clichés come to the rescue.[3] In fact, if one were to collect clichés, like stamps or jokes, one would find a rich field of exploration in obituaries, in letters of condolence, and in funeral orations. It seems as if variations are deemed uncouth, or almost magically harmful and hazardous. Indeed, by leaving the set of clichés in such precarious situations one may easily hurt feelings inadvertently. Hence to abandon the reign of clichés in such circumstances, one might easily and uncontrollably touch and hurt some very deep-seated emotional and irrational layers in people. Clichés help us to stay safely at the surface without, however, appearing to be indifferent.

(The following anecdote may illustrate to what an extent the clichés connected with death have been routinized in our social life. In most Western societies the widow(er) is offered so-called 'heart-felt condolences' directly after the burial of the deceased spouse. I once witnessed on such an occasion in the Netherlands, while lining up with relatives and friends to offer condolences to a widow, how the person in front of me, with tears in her eyes, offered her 'heart-felt congratulations'. (In Dutch the equivalents of 'condolence' and 'congratulation' are even more similar than in English: 'gecondo-leerd' and 'gefeliciteerd'.) The remarkable fact was, however, that the lady did not correct her error, nor did the widow seem to notice it at all. Obviously, she had been firmly programmed to hear the very same cliché over and over again. Incidentally, if death is a rich source for clichés, its opposite, birth, also seems to trigger cliché reactions in an almost mechanical manner. The standard question addressed to parents prior to a birth is whether 'it has to be' a boy or a girl. The standard answer is – at least in most circles of Western, modernized society – that it does not matter 'as long as the baby is healthy'. Generally, birth announcements are as cliché-ridden as death announcements.)

Since situations of precariousness are generally much harder to mend than the previously discussed embarrassing situations, clichés usually stand in need, in this case, of some extra emphasis and of some kind of legitimation. These are bestowed on the clichés by the *authority of specialists*. In the precarious situation of severe illness the doctor, in the precarious situation of death the priest (or the rabbi, or the minister) will bestow the weight of their authority on the clichés, rendering them far more convincing and effective than they would have been, if expressed by 'laymen'. In fact, these holders of 'special' knowledge are often able to render even the bleakest and most hackneyed cliché authoritative and effective.

This mechanism which, it seems to me, is relevant in terms of the sociology of knowledge, works of course also outside the realm of precariousness. For instance, clichés used and expressed by famous politicians and scientists, gain quite similarly in influence and effect. The mechanism can be compared to the ways in which pre-modern priests and magicians, allegedly invested with super-natural power, commanded authoritative, often secret knowledge by means of which they exercised considerable social and sometimes political power.

As in the case of embarrassing situations, laughter may also occur as a kind of pre-reflective response in precarious situations. In his well-known essay on crying and laughter,[4] the German philosopher Helmuth Plessner argues that the laughter elicited by a joke often functions as an answer to a situation which is, in fact, unanswerable. Something happens, or something is being said; the mind is unable to respond adequately; the body assumes command; and the person bursts into uncontrollable laughter. This response is remarkably functional because the only adequate response to laughter is laughter! And laughing together as a group, strengthens the morale, enabling its members to face the threatening situation with more confidence and strength. It is, of course, not a 'real' answer at all, but it does function. The functionality of clichés is very similar to this. They too are not 'real' answers to precarious situations, but they do function, in particular they enable us to continue to communicate, as it were, on the safe surface. Moreover, as in the case of laughter, clichés can only be adequately repaid in kind. Repeating the clichés together, we may render them even more convincing and functional.

Clichés as survivals of magic

Throughout the ages human beings have responded to unanswerable, precarious situations by means of religion and magic. Religion provided the many legitimations of suffering and death (Weber's theodicy), while magic promised to offer techniques for the mobilization of alleged spiritual powers against these life-destroying forces. They thus provided human beings with certainty and managed to comfort them, not in the least by an endless repetition of the same myths, the same formulas, the same rituals. Facing precariousness, this repetitiveness apparently provided man with certainty – as illusory as this certainty may often have been.

In this section, I shall argue in an admittedly somewhat bold hypothesis, that clichés embody survivals of pre-modern magic in a society which is otherwise radically 'disenchanted' (Weber). Or to formulate it differently, in the clichés pre-modern consciousness has been preserved and carried over to modernity. This, I fully realize, is a suggestion which is very hard to prove empirically. It can however, at least be further substantiated and as a substantiated conjecture it may well have its value in the present attempt to understand the cliché as a sociological phenomenon.

A most remarkable feature of clichés is their repetitive and schematic nature. That is, in certain situations and moments of social life, clichés can be expected and if they occur as expected, they usually have the same form and content as before. They are like 'bless you' or '*Gesundheit*' which inevitably, almost instinctively, follows upon a sneeze, or they resemble '*bon appétit*' which necessarily follows after the guests at table have taken up their knife and fork. Clichés can also be likened to the bed-time stories of little children. These stories too have to be repetitive and schematic in form and content. Variations are appreciated since they only emphasize the given structure, but they ought to be minor ones. These repetitive and schematic stories seem to satisfy some very fundamental magical needs in children which in the process of socialization (of growing up in a modern, disenchanted world) will gradually be sublimated. The repetitiveness of institutional behaviour and of clichés are the main sublimations. As modern adults we tend to view ourselves as rationalized and civilized beings who are distinguished in this from children and so-called 'primitives' – a belief very much rooted in the basic tenets and biases of the Enlightenment. It is, however, questionable as to whether we have really evolved beyond the magical needs which we can observe in children and pre-modern 'primitives'. We probably just sublimated these needs in clichés and in institutions which are admittedly far more rational and disenchanted than the magical rites and formulas of the 'primitive' and the repetitive games of the child. This, however, does not at all mean that those magical needs have vanished in modernity.

In this respect, Vilfredo Pareto's distinction between *residues* and *derivations* has great heuristic value. The residues are the vitalistic, non-rational impulses of human behaviour. They are the constants in the development of human civilization. If they change at all, their mutation is very slow and rather minimal. The derivations are the countless rationalizations of these impulses by means of which human beings try to convince themselves and others that they act rationally and purposively. These derivations change all the time. They are, Pareto said, like rubber bands and can be stretched to any length required. Pareto believed that one had to plough through all these often weird and preposterous derivations with the help of what he called the logico-experimental method, in order to arrive at those impulses which drive human beings, their history, and their society. He tried to do this (I believe, unsuccessfully) in the baroque volumes of his *Trattato di Sociologia Generale* – a Promethean search for the elementary structures of human behaviour hidden under the dust of countless ideas, notions, and theories (which frequently have all the features of the cliché). It will not surprise the reader that Pareto paid due attention to magic, viewing it as a very forceful residue of human behaviour. This was taken up again much later by Arnold Gehlen who, in his theory of institutions, viewed magical behaviour as the primeval origin of institutional behaviour.[5]

Meanwhile, the adult use of clichés can also be compared to the child's delight in repetitive and schematic rhymes. In children's rhymes the semantic content of the words is quite obviously irrelevant, particularly if these words are rhythmically accompanied by bodily movements. The sounds of the words, the rhythmic cadence of the phrases, and the movements of the body *fascinate* the child. It is very much a magical fascination which is aroused and satisfied not by meanings but by repetitive and rhythmic sounds and movements – just as is the case in pre-modern, magical rites and formulas. It is the function that counts: these rhymes arouse and satisfy emotions which are part of a deep-seated residual kind of magic.

If one looks at these rhymes reflectively (which only the disenchanted modern adult will do), the content strikes one often as being totally absurd, and sometimes even rather cruel. An example of an absurd and cruel rhyme which is recited to the child while he is being jogged up and down on one's knees, up till the last word, at which moment he is seemingly dropped to the floor, presents the following German song:

> Hoppe, hoppe Reiter,
> wenn er fällt dann schreit er,
> fällt er in den Graben,
> fressen ihn die Raben,
> fällt er in den Sumpf,
> macht der Reiter plumpsch!

The literal translation is: 'Gee-up, gee-up, horseman, when he falls, he shrieks, if he falls in the grave, the raven eats him, if he falls in the swamp, the horseman goes splash!' Significantly, one can easily play this rhyme-game with children who do not understand German at all. The semantic content is obviously irrelevant; it is the words' rhythm, the sentences' schematic structure, and the accompanying bodily movements that fascinate and excite them. This is precisely the same in magic: the sounds of the words in the formulas, the lilt of repetitive vocal and bodily gestures are infinitely more important than semantic meaning.

The clichés of our adult and modern social life do not, of course, arouse the spontaneous gut-reactions which the children's rhymes or the pre-modern, magical rites and formulas seem to trigger. We exchange our clichés in a seemingly rational attitude of 'matter-of-factness' (Weber; Mannheim). At most we feel uncomfortable when someone refuses to 'play the game' and constantly tries to avoid the use of clichés. Such a person irritates and confuses us, and thus seems to touch some deep-seated emotions. Yet, despite the fact that clichés cannot realistically be viewed as sources and targets of magical fascination and enchantment (that would indeed be stretching the argument too far), they seem to constitute survivals of magical techniques by which human beings, throughout the ages, have satisfied some deep-seated needs for security, stability and certainty. Apparently, these needs cannot be sufficiently satisfied on the level of meaning alone. Throughout the ages, they have been satisfied primarily in a mechanistic and functional manner, and clichés very much belong to this tradition. Their repetitiveness, their predictability, their recognizability, their applicability – with the exclusion of a reflective pondering of meaning – provide our interactions and communication in social life with a mechanic stability which may very well satisfy unobtrusively and thus the more effectively some deep-seated, residually magical needs. This, it seems to me, is in itself a rather enchanting idea: disguised as taken-for-granted clichés, magic seems to peep through the crevices of our modern, disenchanted and supposedly civilized society.

Clichés and mobilization

As meaningless as they may actually be, if taken to the letter, clichés are yet able to arouse behaviour as in a stimulus–response sequence. As we have seen in chapter 1, they share this characteristic with slogans. This is probably the most important function of the cliché. It manages to trigger speech and behaviour, while the potentially relativizing influence of cognitive reflection is evaded – or, perhaps better, passed by. In this section our discussion of this mobilizing function will focus mainly on the sectors of commerce (cf. advertising slogans), while the next section will be devoted entirely to a discussion of the mobilizing function in politics.

To begin with, one should realize that this behaviouristic trigger-function is by no means obvious. It is so hard to recognize the mobilizing effect on our speech and behaviour, precisely because cognitive reflections are – if rather unobtrusively–evaded. Second, slogans and clichés do not directly trigger speech and behaviour, but rather influence attitudes, tendencies, moods. The slogan of a commercial, to give an obvious example, does not affect the behaviour of the housewife in such a way that she runs off to the shop immediately to buy the commodities advertized. Likewise, the clichés of a political speech do not directly cause people to vote for one politician and not for another. Rather slogans and clichés mould people's attitudes and moods; they prepare them for a certain course of cognition, emotion and action; they try to arouse the desire to buy an advertised product or to vote for a promulgated political programme. Thus, the clichés of a political speech try to convince people unobtrusively that the general content of the proposed political course is 'naturally' and 'obviously' the only correct one. Above all, they try to convince the individuals in their audience that most people think, feel and act this way, and that one should 'obviously' not be so silly as to deviate from this trend.

To use an admittedly somewhat loaded expression, clichés try to influence people rather like brainwashing. They seem to carry truth – an old and an obvious truth – not because of their semantic content but because of their repetitive use. They are usually not heuristically convincing (that would require a reflective pondering of their meaning), but they are magically convincing i.e. produce a sort of enchantment (which needs an emotional participation in the general cadence of the words, the sounds and the bodily movements).

One of the main reasons that clichés manage to evade reflection and its potential relativizations, lies in the fact that they are as catching as laughter, or if you want, as stuttering. If one talks to someone who stutters badly, one really has to control one's own speech, lest one begin to stutter also. Likewise, if there is any sociological law of imitation, it certainly applies to laughter. The same mechanism is at work in the use of clichés. They are uncontrollably exchanged in the countless interactions of daily social life, and we rarely realize that one cliché seems to call, well-nigh instinctively, for the next one.

If it is correct, as I argued in chapter 2, following some very fundamental theorems of Gehlen and Schelsky, that modern society fosters permanent reflection (*Dauerreflexion*), the avoidance of this cognitive reflection by the use of clichés becomes especially important. Or, if Thomas was right when he wrote that there are many rival definitions of the situation in modern society, none of which is binding anymore, clichés may gain sociological importance since they manage to by-pass the many rival definitions and influence human speech and behaviour, as it were, beyond these definitions. They do not, of course, create a moral bond, but they do tie people to certain courses of behaviour in a more mechanical and 'behaviouristic' way.

Being catching is, of course, not sufficient for this mobilizing function of clichés. They have to be presented in a special way – repetitively and hyperbolically. The modern mass media are quite instrumental in this respect. They are able to bombard people loudly and on a massive scale with commercial and political slogans over and over again, gradually making everyone immune to reflection on the semantic content of these slogans. The slogans and clichés of commerce and politics are indeed often rude and loud, and very hyperbolic in expression. They try to shock, to jolt people out of the inertia that results from permanent reflection, without allowing them however to reflectively ponder on their semantic content.

Intellectuals occupy a special position in this respect, since they tend to reflect more often and more critically than the other social categories and classes in modern society. As a result, commercial and political clichés that try to mobilize prospective intellectual 'customers', will have to make a special effort in this circumvention of cognitive reflection. In short, to be effective the slogans and clichés geared to intellectuals will have to be blatantly hyperbolic. I tested this hypothesis by the following simple, admittedly non-representative, yet illuminating experiment.

From all the issues of the *New York Review of Books* that appeared in 1976, I took at random the issue 24 June (vol. 23, no. 11) and analysed the twenty-one book advertisements. I then selected the adjectives which seemed to make an effort to stimulate some kind of emotion. Meanwhile, one should realize that the market to which the publishers address themselves in these advertisements consists predominantly of supposedly *critical* intellectuals on an *academic* level. Allegedly, the adjectives of these commercials, which one can find in many other book advertisements, do work on these intellectuals.

The majority of all the adjectives used were of a hyperbolic nature. I recorded the following (the number in parentheses refers to the page in the mentioned issue of the *Review*): fascinating (2), extraordinary, electrifying (5), fascinating (6), fascinating, explosive, sweeping, stimulating, suggestive, marvellous, marvellously (7), electrifying (10), marvellous, terrifying, sensational, devastating, absorbing, disarming, shocking, fascinating, exciting, electrifying, menacing, devastating, moving, marvellous (13), interesting (14), revealing, challenging (15), illuminating (18), dazzling, stimulating, imposing, startling (20), incomparable (23), stimulating, fascinating, exhilirating (29), astounding (30), incisive (31), penetrating, candid and intriguing (32), bewildering (34), excellent (37), extraordinary, astonishing (44). It seems as if these hyperbolic adjectives try to work the intellectuals of the book market into a magical frenzy: shocking, electrifying, exhilirating, dazzling, compelling – and, of course, in a case of magic – fascinating. They are all typically cliché, repetitive, meaningless to the letter, but apparently functional.

In the advertisements analysed research is 'extensive' (16), a study is 'definitive' (16), or 'detailed and comprehensive' (20), a literary figure 'leading' (18), a book 'acclaimed' (29), an insight 'perceptive' (30), a view 'revealing' (34), a variety 'bewildering' (34), a wisdom 'accumulated' (34), an account 'incisive' (31). The advertised books are not just remarkable but 'most remarkable' (18); not just promising, but 'most promising' (27); not just significant, but 'most significant' (15). Indeed, they are 'magnificently illustrated' (5), 'most intimately autobiographical' (7), 'truly sensational' (13), 'totally absorbing' (13), 'marvellously helpful' (7), 'extremely candid' (18).

Finally, the authors of these products receive qualifications which should make them blush: 'one of the great scholars of our age' (5), 'one of the most important names in twentieth-century philosophy' (5), 'a revolutionary in the best tradition' (15), 'one of the very best living American writers' (18).

In sum, one gets very dizzy, if one reads these advertisements attentively i.e. reflectively, but one is not, of course, supposed to do that at all. These widely and repetitively distributed adjectives should by-pass reflection and semi-magically enchant the reader. The aim of this enchantment is simply that the reader should gradually feel *compelled* to read and thus to buy these books. The medium of television commands special techniques of enchantment which greatly enhance the mobilizing function of the commercial cliché. I am not just referring to the obvious cliché lady in evening-gown, sensually caressing the newest brand of car. Much more unobtrusively magical are specific close-up techniques and the various forms of accompanying music – sometimes loud and harsh (e.g. when hamburgers or chicken are to be consumed), sometimes soft and seductive (e.g. when bath oil or perfumes are to be sold). It is as if the clichés of these commercials try to enter into us, through the eyes and the ears, touching our emotions while by-passing our cognitive faculties. Indeed, analysing them cognitively, commercials appear to be bluntly stupid. Their producers know this perfectly well, of course. But then, they do not want to satisfy our minds. On the contrary, they try to by-pass the mind as far as possible in order to influence prospective customers behaviouristically in an unreflective stimulus–response sequence. To this end, clichés are indispensable.

Clichés and propaganda

It stands to reason that clichés have always been instrumental in conveying propaganda. The aim of all forms of propaganda, whether religious or secular–political, is to penetrate through the shield of existing ideas and convictions, and to instil in human beings different ideas and convictions. Propaganda bombards individuals widely and repetitively with 'information', containing the clichés of the propagated ideology. It is hoped that their minds will eventually yield to them, stop reflecting on, and be moulded by them.

Historically, propaganda was for the first time officially instituted in 1622 by Pope Gregory XV in the famous *Congregatio de Propaganda Fidei*, apparently as part of the Counter-Reformation. In the beginning the congregation consisted of a group of cardinals who supervised foreign missions, and bore responsibility for the training of missionaries. Ever since, propaganda-clichés have constituted an important part of both Roman-Catholic and Protestant brands of Christian doctrine. In modern times, these clichés have been cast quite often in commercial-like slogans. Huge banners with slogans saying 'Jesus is the Lord', or 'Jesus, Our Lord and Saviour', not only decorate revivalist meetings, like those of Billy Graham (who, incidentally, has understood the power of clichés perfectly), but also the usually more austere meetings of the World Council of Churches. Meanwhile, as is the case with all clichés, one should not reflectively ponder upon their precise meaning.

Recently, billboards appeared at some roadsides in the USA saying: 'I have found it!' These words supposedly carry some kind of religious message. In terms of our present discussion of clichés and propaganda, this slogan presents an interesting case. Strictly speaking, the slogan does not carry any semantic content and its aim is, obviously, to trigger instead of to avoid reflection. Therefore, it is certainly not a cliché. The driver in his car who has read the slogan, is supposed to ask himself such questions as: 'Did *I* find it?', 'Did I find *what*?', 'What am I supposed to find?' It remains rather doubtful, whether such a semantically empty slogan will yield any of the intended results. It may indeed trigger some reflection, but these thoughts are doomed to remain gratuitous and uncommitted, and will easily float away from religious to more mundane concerns.

Modern propaganda is most eminent in politics. It reached its first height of expertise in Nazi Germany, where even the most incredible clichés (so dear and in fact indispensable to any totalitarian system) gained credibility and legitimacy through the power and charisma of the leader(s), as well as through such totalitarian and manipulatory techniques as mass gatherings and military parades. Modern political propaganda reached a further technical perfection during the so-called Cold War. Increasingly, propaganda specialists began to apply scientific techniques, drawn from psychological behaviourism and depth-psychology. Its most typical characteristic is the attempt to influence people, not with the spectacular 'pomp and circumstance' of fascist totalitarianism, but by much more unobtrusive methods, massaging people's consciousness incessantly rather like brainwashing. The ideological clichés of the Cold War, deemed essential and fundamental to the human species, were repeated over and over again: 'the free world', 'capitalist decadence', 'better dead than red', 'imperialist repression' – and, jointly on all political fronts: 'democracy'. The semantic emptiness of these clichés is quite functional, since it can be used for political manipulation. A good example presents the juxtaposition 'left/ right', and 'progressive/conservative'. If one brackets one's personal political convictions for a moment and looks at these concepts more closely, one is bound to be at a loss as to their precise meaning. In fact, some twenty years ago all military regimes in the world were notoriously 'right' and 'conservative', if not 'reactionary' and 'fascist'. Today, there are several military regimes which profess to be, and indeed are announced by journalists as being 'left' and 'progressive'. Have these military leaders really moved to a progressive, socially just policy, or do they make political capital out of clichés which better fit the general political mood of the present? Or, to take another example, terrorists usually claim to fight for a 'progressive' and 'left' cause. Would they have been 'left' in Italy or Germany during the 1930s and early 1940s? Or the so-called dissidents in Eastern Europe, are they 'left' or 'right', 'progressive' or 'conservative', or perhaps 'conservative-here' and 'progressive-there'? Or just the other way about? Ulbricht called himself and the country he ruled tyrannically 'democratic', while Hitler saw himself and his Nazi movement as being 'socialist'. If taken to the letter, such clichés remain semantically empty. But then, one should not try to pin clichés down semantically – certainly not in the case of politics. There clichés can be given any meaning, and that is precisely the reason why they are so eminently useful in political manipulations. George Orwell expressed this some thirty years ago in his well-known essay 'Politics and the English Language' (1946). He stressed in particular the political importance of the semantic vagueness of clichés:[6]

The word 'Fascism' has now no meaning except in so far as it signifies 'something not desirable'. The words 'democracy', 'socialism', 'freedom', patriotic', 'realistic', 'justice' have each of them several different meanings which cannot be reconciled with one another. In the case of a word like 'democracy', not only is there no agreed definition, but the attempt to make one is resisted from all sides. It is almost universally felt that when we call a country democratic we are praising it: consequently the defenders of every kind of régime claim that it is a democracy, and fear that they might have to stop using the word if it were tied down to any one meaning. Words of this kind are often used in a consciously dishonest way. That is, the person who uses them has his own private definition, but allows his hearer to think he means something quite different. Statements like 'Marshal Pétain was a true patriot', 'The Soviet press is the freest in the world', 'The Catholic Church is opposed to persecution', are always made with intent to deceive. Other words used in variable meanings, in most cases more or less dishonestly, are: 'class', 'totalitarian', 'science', 'progressive', 'reactionary', 'bourgeois', 'equality'.

The late Dutch sociologist A. N. J. den Hollander once described these political clichés aptly as 'dead word-cartridges with which the political sorcerers produce a ghostly rattling'.[7] Fowler summed it up when he wrote:[8]

> Clichés are plentiful in the linguistic currency of politics, domestic and international. They too, however happy in their original application, soon lose any semantic value they may have had, and become almost wholly emotive. That, for instance, has been the fate of 'self-determination', 'appeasement', 'power politics', 'parity of esteem', 'underprivileged classes', 'victimization', and innumerable others, including 'democracy' itself, the classic example of a Humpty-Dumpty word. Even those admirable recent coinages 'cold war', 'iron curtain', 'peaceful coexistence' and 'wind of change' are now so near to clichés as to offer themselves to substitutes for thought. It has been said by one who ought to know that 'When Mr. Krushschev says "peaceful coexistence" he means almost precisely what we mean by "cold war"'.

Clichés and social control

It may be stated as a kind of cultural rule that we have gained full command over a foreign language when we are able to tell jokes in it, and when we can discern clichés as indeed being clichés i.e. as worn-out and hackneyed phrases or instances of behaviour. Sociologically this means that both jokes and clichés may function as criteria by which 'natives' and 'strangers', 'insiders' and 'outsiders' can be distinguished and, if need be, separated. This obviously entails again a strong mechanism of social control: the jokes and clichés not only keep certain individuals and collectivities outside the group, they simultaneously keep the members of the group within its boundaries.[9]

The Biblical passage Judges 12:4–6 relates the socio-linguistically interesting story of the Gileadites who had an ingenious method unmasking any fugitive from Ephraim with which they were at war. They would ask a fugitive Ephraimite to say 'Shibboleth' and when he pronounced it like 'Sibboleth' – which Ephraimites apparently always did – he would be taken and slain. Likewise, during the Second World War, members of the Dutch Resistance were allegedly able to detect German infiltrators by asking suspicious-looking individuals to say 'Scheveningen' – the name of a town – very few people outside Holland are able to pronounce it correctly: a real 'shibboleth'. In this sense, the clichés of every language are the shibboleths of that language and its surrounding culture. Likewise,

71

the professional groups and the various sub-cultures within a country or specific society – from professionals with their jargon, to thieves with their specific argot, to youth gangs with their particular slang – have their own clichés which function as shibboleths and form a kind of cultural wall around the collectivity.

It stands to reason that clichés control the members of such groups in an unobtrusive, yet pervasive manner. As we have seen repeatedly, clichés are the moulds or casts of consciousness, which influence speech and behaviour with the exclusion of cognitive reflection – thus, with the exclusion of potential relativizations. This, of course, is of eminent importance in modern society in which values, norms, meanings and motives have the tendency to float freely in thin, morally ambiguous, social air. In such a situation, as we have seen, clichés are able to take over the social control functions which the traditional institutions seem to lose increasingly. In short, as unimaginative and reified in nature as they may have become, clichés provide the modern individual, in a very unobtrusive manner, with some degree of clarity, stability and certainty, while they also exert a social control which he will in no way experience as oppressive or repressive because he is hardly aware of its existence and pervasiveness.

Conclusion

The discussion of this chapter focused exclusively on the main social and political functions of clichés. There are, of course, more and other functions – perhaps no less interesting and important – but they fall outside the sociological scope of the present study. For example, one could perhaps compare the clichés psychoanalytically with dreams and wit, both of which possess, according to Freud, some very basic psychological functions. A Freudian would probably discuss clichés as part of the 'psycho-pathology of everyday life'. Or, to take another example, the clichés may well function psychologically in what Fowler has called 'irrelevant allusions'.[10] By this he meant that we often talk in daily social life in sentences which in part are perfectly 'normal' but consist for the other part of a hackneyed phrase which is irrelevant in the context of that sentence, but which has been admitted by sheer force of association. Irrelevant allusions occur, according to Fowler, 'when one draws our attention to the methodical by telling us there is "method in the madness", though method not madness is all there is to see, when another's every winter is "the winter of his discontent", when a third cannot complain of the light without calling it "religious" as well as "dim", when for a fourth nothing can be rotten except "in the state of Denmark".'[11] Psychologically, clichés can indeed be seen very much as mental moulds, as routinely engraved paths which our speech easily, pre-reflectively follows, even on the slightest suggestion and even if following a given path or route does not make any sense. But again, these are psychological dimensions that cannot concern us too much in the present sociological analysis of clichés.

It will also be clear that the discussed social and political functions can and will occur in all sectors of society and that we cannot engage here in a systematic treatment of all of them. Such a discussion would, for a considerable part, consist of an analysis of the various kinds of argot, jargon or slang being used in these sectors.

However, in conclusion, we ought to devote a few more observations to the phenomenon of jargon. The term 'jargon' usually refers to the written and/or spoken language of certain specialists in the various societal sectors – a language which is generally deemed to be rather ugly-sounding and on the whole quite incomprehensible.[12] Fowler named a few examples: 'legalese', commercialese', 'officialese' and 'sociologese'. Naturally, jargon is quite prone to develop standard expressions which are semantically poor but which the specialists keep repeating, like sorcerers repetitively reciting their sacred formulas. By doing so, they may successfully create the illusion in themselves as well as in others that the words spoken and/or written are relevant, important, worthwhile, etc. That is, the jargon of modern specialists is inescapably cliché-ridden.

The sociological discipline exhibits perhaps more than any other science or humanity – with the exception of psychology, I believe – the clichégenic nature of its jargon. What precisely is the meaning of such endlessly repeated, and admittedly often unavoidable, concepts as 'structure', 'function', 'social', 'cultural', 'dynamic', 'static', 'empirical' and above all 'dialectic', this sociological 'Humpty Dumpty word' (Fowler)? In the course of a sociological discussion such concepts can be provided with more precise meanings, but this is usually not done and one may strongly suspect that such an omission is intentional. In that case, these and other concepts are blatant clichés which together make up a conceptually abstruse jargon: sociologese. With his customary wit, Fowler has perceived the true nature and origin of this jargon clearly and mercilessly:[13]

Sociology is a new science concerning itself not with esoteric matters outside the comprehension of the layman, as the older sciences do, but with the ordinary affairs of ordinary people. This seems to engender in those who write about it a feeling that the lack of any abstruseness in their subject demands a compensatory abstruseness in their language. Thus, in the field of industrial relations, what the ordinary man would call an informal talk may be described as a 'relatively unstructured conversational interaction', and its purpose may be said to be 'to build, so to speak, within the mass of demand and need, a framework of limitation recognized by both worker and client'. This seems to mean that the client must be persuaded that, beyond a certain point, he can only rely on what used to be called self-help; but that would not sound a bit scientific.

4 Clichés and boredom
The supersedure of meaning by function in the experience of time

Introduction[1]

When a society grows abstract, when individuals are no longer able to meaningfully relate to institutions and traditional social and moral bonds in a taken-for-granted manner, behavioural problems such as *alienation* and *anomie* will be paired with *boredom*. In the wake of Marxist and Durkheimian sociological thought, alienation and anomie have attracted much sociological attention, but most sociologists have failed to view boredom as a relevant sociological problem, rooted in the historically specific constitution of modern society. The reason for this neglect lies partly in the fact that the general methodological thrust of contemporary sociology prevents most of its experts from seeing and then defining a culturally conditioned phenomenon like boredom as a sociological fact. It has been difficult but apparently not impossible to operationalize alienation and anomie, and to empirically study them within the premises of neo-positivist research. The question is, however, whether the original Marxist and Durkheimian content of meaning has not evaporated in the process. Similarly, one can conceivably construct a boredom-scale, but the results of such a research technique would probably be trivial in the end effect, and totally neglect the gist of the present argument.

In this chapter I shall argue that the supersedure of meaning by function which I have constantly viewed as the fundamental feature of modernization, has had a strong impact on the *experience of time* by modern man. That is, in a fully modernized society, ruled by the many regulations of bureaucracy and thoroughly rationalized in a functional manner, time-awareness is almost totally absorbed by clock-time ('objective time'), while time as an ongoing, pre-reflectively experienced duration ('subjective time'), founded on a meaningful tradition, related to institutions and borne by meaningful bonds (cf. the pre-modern ritual calendar), dwindles and atrophies. It is a supersedure of subjective time by objective time. Indeed, 'I don't have time' and 'time is money' are two significant modern clichés which point at this supersedure in modern man's time-awareness. People in modern society are always busy. They fill up their clock-time with countless actions which are predominantly functionally rational. However, not being able to experience time also as an ongoing, meaningful stream – Bergson's *durée* – coming from a past, heading for a future, they will increasingly experience *boredom*, despite the fact that they are often very busy and generally object to being lazy (cf. so-called Protestant ethics).

I shall not use boredom here in the superficial sense of 'not knowing what to do with one's time'. This very real boredom exists when one does not know how to fill one's clock-time. Children experience it quite often. It also presents a gigantic problem for many adults in modern society, particularly in the cases of unemployment and relatively early (often compulsory) retirement. I rather want to probe beyond this obvious kind of boredom, and sociologically analyse that kind of boredom which is related to the experience of subjective time and lies at the very foundation of modern society and modern consciousness. As such, it affects rather unobtrusively also those people who are busily employed and thus very much able to fill up their clock-time.

When the modern individual is no longer able pre-reflectively to relate to his surrounding institutions, that is, when he permanently reflects about meanings and values and no definition of the situation seems to be morally binding anymore, his subjective time will have lost its co-ordinates: there is no past to which to relate meaningfully, no future to focus meaningfully upon (Gehlen's *post-histoire*). In such a situation, subjective time floats on in a void and will be superseded easily by the functionality of clock-time. Perhaps, modern man keeps himself functionally busy, driven by a compulsive work-ethos, because his subjective time has atrophied. In sum, when, due to modernization, the *durée* of modern man loses its traditional and institutional co-ordinates, he may be able to fill up his clock-time busily and compulsively (and become frightened, if he is prevented from doing so i.e. by unemployment, or retirement), but he will experience, on the level of subjective time, a very pervasive *ennui*. Time then lasts an awfully long while: *Langeweile*. At the same time, however, time floating on without institutional co-ordinates (e.g. without traditionally accepted and meaningfully experienced *rites de passage* which indicate the different stages in the ongoing life of the individual as an intrinsic part of a social collectivity),[2] will not only last a long while but also be experienced as running very fast. The cliché 'I ran out of time' is usually meant in terms of clock-time. The modern individual, however, experiences it also in terms of subjective time. The compulsive pace at which the modern man performs his functions within the strictures of clock-time should be correlated to the feeling that life rushes by at a corresponding pace.

In sum, boredom will be viewed here as a typically modern characteristic of the experience of subjective time. The two main characteristics of this boredom are that subjective time is experienced as lasting an endlessly long while, and the simultaneous experience that it runs at a fast pace. Both characteristics have been caused by the supersedure of meaning by function which, in terms of time, entails a supersedure of subjective time by objective time.

Clichés, it will be argued in this chapter, are the perfect moulds of consciousness for this kind of boredom. As we saw in chapter 1, clichés may be seen as chunks of past experience in which time has been frozen. As such, they can function as substitutes for the lacking institutional co-ordinates. In the cultural void, caused by the super-sedure of meaning by function, clichés will provide points of orientation which are readily acceptable (i.e. without relativizing reflections). Clichés will, of course, not remove or abolish boredom, rather they provide this pervasive and necessarily vague kind of boredom with forms of expression, enabling individuals to maintain a functional interaction with their fellow human beings. In other words, boredom on the level of subjective time may become socially destructive, incapacitating individuals from communicating, from interacting. Baudelaire who perhaps more than anyone else experienced this kind of *ennui*, warned that a bored individual would unscrupulously destroy the whole world, if he could.[3] Clichés bind people to the past and enable them to maintain a minimum of interaction, as functional as this interaction may be.

However, clichés may themselves become boring. Having been repeated over and over again, the clichés may, at any given moment, emphasize the fact that they are actually mere substitutes, that modern subjective time has definitely lost its meaningful co-ordinates, that life just floats on meaninglessly and aimlessly. Individuals who experience this are liable to be unwilling to repeat the clichés in their speech and behaviour any longer. They may then easily engage in aggressive and often bizarre acts – very much the fate of the clichés of political ideologies. Although one must add the element of power-lessness (which we will discuss in this chapter), boredom *vis-à-vis* political clichés is certainly to be viewed in terms of atrophied subjective time. The individual who participates, in speech and behaviour, in the prolongation of a political ideology, is liable to be sooner or later bored by its clichés. He will then have to make a decision: either he abandons the ideology, or he tries to enact it, beyond the clichés, in deeds of aggression. Much (but, of course, not all) of contemporary political violence can be explained in these terms.

Since the connection between clichés, boredom and aggression is not at all obvious, I have used this introduction to present it in outline, and shall try, in what now follows, to further substantiate this point.

The sociological dimensions of subjective time

It is in human behaviour that subjective time becomes concrete – i.e. measurable and observable. Human behaviour occurs in countless *situations* which have a certain time span, a beginning and an end. Although they constitute social life as in an ongoing stream, they can be recalled from memory as distinct units, and they can, in principle, be enacted at any time in reality. They are concrete to such an extent that we can give them names: 'hunt', 'harvest', 'prayer', 'discussion', 'lecture', 'football game', etc. We can even measure their duration in terms of clock-time.

These situations demarcate the limits of behaviour. We know how we have to behave when we want to conduct a discussion – we know the rules that are to be obeyed and the values that we must believe in, if we want a fruitful and meaningful discussion. Without such situations, behaviour would just float on in time – without motives, without purposes, without past or future. That is, behaviour would be imperilled.

Because of these situations, human thoughts, emotions and actions do not occur capriciously and on the spur of the moment – as is often the case with instinctive behaviour which is clearly situationless. On the contrary, human behaviour extends between a remembered past (before we began to discuss, we remembered what a discussion is like i.e. how it is being socially defined), and a projected future (we engage in the discussion with an aim in mind). This memory and this projection are not private and individual, but collective and social processes. The definitions of situations contain collective norms, values and meanings which have been learned in socialization and passed on from generation to generation in tradition.

However, in the historically specific context of modern, *abstract* society these characteristics of situations and situational behaviour have changed rather dramatically. In this society, to quote Thomas once more, there are many definitions of the situation, but none of them is binding. Due to this pluralism, the ties between traditional norms, values and meanings on the one hand and individual behaviour on the other loosen. Behaviour will remain functionally predictable (cf. bureaucratic rules) to a very large degree, but beneath this functional level, it will grow morally unstable. That means, wherever behaviour is not totally absorbed by fixed routines (bureaucracy cannot control the whole of social and individual life), it will tend to occur semi-instinctively on the spur of the moment. Similarly, while objective clock-time will strictly regiment modern behaviour, the subjective time beneath this functional level will increasingly atrophy in modern, abstract society. No longer tied to the situational norms, values and meanings of traditional institutions, modern man will increasingly experience subjective time as an aimless, rapid stream, without a past to remember and a future to expect. He lives in the here-and-now with an attitude that Weber and Mannheim have called the 'pragmatic matter-of-factness'.

These, then, are the sociological ingredients of boredom. A bored individual will behave erratically, on the spur of the moment, whenever he is not functionally regimented. His words, thoughts, emotions and actions are not coherently related: a bored individual may think and feel one thing, and suddenly do something quite different; one day he may say he believes in something, the next day he may well do the very opposite. He will also consume rather erratically: bored as he is, he will aimlessly eat and buy a great deal. That is, outside the firmly regimented spheres of his life (particularly in his leisure time), the bored individual will talk and behave quite erratically. It stands to reason that such erratic behaviour is quite common today in the so-called 'free professions', since human life is much less regimented here. In particular modern artists, writers, musicians and academicians often display a kind of behaviour which demonstrates a very deep-seated boredom.

Not surprisingly, bored individuals will complain much of alienation. Before we discuss the sociologically very important relationship between boredom and loss of power, we must deal briefly with the intrinsic bond between boredom and alienation.

Boredom and alienation

When the gods are being banished from the earth, Hegel once said, the reign of boredom begins.[4] Hegel distinguished two large periods of boredom in Occidental history. The first period occurred when the Romans occupied the nations around the Mediterranean and the national gods began to lose their hold on their believers, since an alien and meaningless power seemed obviously to be much stronger than they. The second period of Occidental boredom set in when the Reformation shattered the medieval *Corpus Christianum*. The boredom caused by Roman imperialism had been driven away by Christianity. The church sacralized nature and society, and provided a religious meaning to the polity. The Reformation, however, tore this meaningful *Gestalt* asunder, threw the individual back on his private conscience, and thus delivered him, according to Hegel, to boredom. The Protestant has left the beauty and holiness of the Middle Ages, and is ever more immersed in the dreariness of the routines of everyday life. There he can only experience boredom – a very pervasive boredom which could only be driven out by a third religion or world-view, succeeding the world-views of the *Imperium Romanum* and the Roman Catholic Church. Hegelianism, we may assume, was the most suitable candidate.

Historically, it is quite likely that boredom played a predominant role in the Hellenistic culture of the Roman empire, the culture of a repressive, uniform state and society. This boredom was very much paired with alienation, as is demonstrated by Gnosticism, a widely spread Hellenistic world-view (divided over many sects and schools of thought).[5] Underlying all forms of Gnosticism is the search for the allegedly redeeming spark of divine light, believed to reside in the depth of the human soul. In his subjectivistic thrust, the Gnostic views the body as the material prison of the spiritual soul and rejects the traditional institutions, since they allegedly alienate man's pure existence. The Gnostic goes in search of absolute meaning, absolute freedom, absolute truth, and absolute time – that is, meaning, freedom, truth and time which are not mediated by the body and the traditional institutions (those objectifying sources of alienation), but ought to be sought for in the depth of the psyche and in the eternity of the cosmos beyond history and society. Since tradition and the values and meanings of existing institutions are not allowed to stimulate the individual's behaviour, in his search for the absolute the Gnostic is bound to rely on all kinds of artificial sources of stimulation: drugs, frantic (often crudely erotic) rituals, wild fantasies, erratic theories, all sorts of emotional 'kicks' – in fact, everything qualifies that manages to titillate the mind and the soul. It stands to reason that this subjectivistic search is doomed only to enhance the feeling of alienation for which, of course, the institutions are blamed again.

Gnosticism, as a radically subjectivistic anti-institutionalism, is more than a Hellenistic phenomenon. The Gnostic is a cultural archetype of Western civilization: the absolutist who rejects the fact that his world has been moulded by former generations (tradition), who rebels against the collective values and norms which both stimulate and control his behaviour (institutions), who searches restlessly for emotional and irrational 'kicks', and loves to dwell in the a-social and a-historical abodes of his subjectivism.[6]

In the history of Christianity, Gnosticism has always been part of socio-political protest movements against the church and its power. It provided the anti-institutional mood suitable for the political conflict against Rome: the Albigenses of Languedoc and Thomas Muenzer's movement are obvious examples. Gnosticism has, of course, also been very close to mysticism (Eckhart). Meanwhile, in its revolt against the Church of Rome, the Reformation has always stressed ecclesiology in order to avoid the heresy of Gnosticism. Nevertheless, much Gnosticism emanated from it. Ever since Romanticism (cf. Goethe's *Faust*), Gnosticism has kept a strong, although secularized, hold on modernity. Hegel's philosophy is strongly Gnostic: it describes the Gnostic 'trip' of the spirit arriving at absolute purity (subjectivity) through its dialectic alienation in objectivity. This Gnostic scheme of thought (the 'dialectical method') was taken over by Marx. Indeed, Marxism is very strongly imbued with Gnosticism. The communist society after the world revolution (in itself a Gnostic event) is a Gnostic's paradise in which no alienation (the Gnostic disease *par excellence*, already diagnosed in Hellenism) will spoil man's absolute freedom.

Gnostic elements are apparent in Freud's psycho-analysis, whereas Jung's depth-psychology is explicitly and essentially Gnostic by nature. Quite interesting are the Gnostic mixtures of Freud and Marx as in the writings of Marcuse and Fromm. Gnosticism, incidentally, has always been prone to syncretisms of an Hellenistic dimension. As long as it titillates his absolutist and subjectivist fantasies, the Gnostic will (usually quite eclectically) embrace any theory, doctrine or world-view.

Alienation may indeed be more than the imaginary disease of Gnostics who have projected it on to history and society out of their impotent subjectivism. Yet their irrational anti-institutionalism is certainly not the way to cure it. One thing, however, is sure: by turning away from tradition and the institutions the Gnostic is doomed to end up in a very deep-seated boredom. Since his organism is not a self-reloading battery, his wild emotions and erratic theories will inevitably dry up and eventually yield only boring clichés. The Gnostic will then either withdraw into lethargy, or indulge in bizarre or even aggressive and violent behaviour.

Boredom and loss of power

In his remarkable study *Melancholie und Gesellschaft* (1969), the German sociologist Wolf Lepenies analyses historically and sociologically the correlation between melancholy and boredom on the one hand, and political and social structures on the other. Whenever human beings are excluded from political power (that is, from the chance to influence politically the behaviour of others), they will, according to Lepenies, withdraw into melancholic moods, become lethargic and generally suffer from boredom. Using a term coined by Arnold Gehlen, Lepenies calls this state of affairs a 'decline of behaviour' (*Handlungsverlust*).

In order to substantiate this, he analysed the power relations at the absolutist courts of Louis XIII and Louis XIV in France. Lepenies distinguishes two systems of order: the primary system consisting of the institutionalized distribution of real political power, centring around the absolute monarch; the secondary system made up of countless privileges, values, norms, and behavioural regulations (the so-called *etiquette*) which tell people at court how to think, feel and act – how to behave. Most courtiers lived in the secondary system which was totally dependent on the primary and it lacked real, political influence. It thus strongly stimulated lethargy, fatalism, melancholy and boredom.

Gradually, two types of reaction developed in this secondary system: aesthetic resignation and political activism. An example of the latter was the Fronde of the second half of the seventeenth century. It was an ill-conceived, planless revolt against the primary system, staged by the powerless nobility and magistracy. Typically, it did not yield any political fruits, except that it enlarged the monarch's power and established a kind of equilibrium between the primary and secondary systems of order. From now on, melancholy and boredom were predominant in the secondary system. Aesthetic resignation became the dominant mode of behaviour: one tried to expel melancholy and boredom by the enjoyment of literature and music (as well as by the cultivation of romantic, erotic, courtly love, we may add: getting involved in love affairs is a favourite pastime of bored people). Lepenies mentions at this point the *salon* as a significant institution. It was a place outside the court where courtiers could enjoy literature, art and music without the interference of the primary system of order. In fact, the monarch – the cause of their melancholy and boredom – was obtrusively absent.

We cannot discuss here the further historical and sociological development of Western boredom. It would be interesting to analyse the bourgeoisification of boredom, the more so since the bourgeoisie originally launched a headstrong attack on the 'decadent' boredom of the nobility. Also, the ultimate of bourgeois boredom – romantic *ennui* – and its institutionalization in nineteenth century dandyism deserves special attention but cannot be discussed here. I would now rather like to apply briefly Lepenies's historical–sociological observation to the context of modern, abstract society.

The individual in most Western modern societies receives delegated power, unless he belongs to the political élite. This delegation of power is carried out and supervised by democratic institutions:

the legislature, the judiciary and the executive. However, like other institutions in modern society, these traditional guardians of democracy and of the democratic distribution of power, have become bureaucratized, specialized and complex to such a degree that most private citizens are unable these days to relate cognitively and emotively to them. To the average citizen, these traditionally divided sectors of power – not to speak of their many invisible coalitions with various economic and military powers – have become abstract and removed structures. He can see, for example, the face of his president or prime minister daily in the newspapers or on television, yet this democratic leader is infinitely more faceless to him than the most feudal monarch was to his subjects in a medieval kingdom. As a result, political participation of civilians – the very cornerstone of democracy ever since the Greek *polis* – has become highly problematic in modern society. This, of course, seriously affects the democratic legitimation of power – a very basic aspect of Nisbet's 'twilight of authority' in our times.

In short, it is hard nowadays for most people to view their ballot as a viable share of political power. To many of us, abstract society constitutes politically a rather undemocratic system in which the average individual is powerless. If Lepenies's hypothesis is correct, such a situation must cause a pervasive boredom which again must give rise to two behavioural reactions: aesthetic resignation and planless, often irrational political activism. In the 1960s and early 1970s adolescents and the younger intelligentsia (artists, teachers and academicians) in most Western countries have indeed, and often loudly, complained about the discrepancy between the power of a relatively small élite – government, business, military – and the powerlessness of the people. Quite characteristically, these Western 'dissidents' engaged in aesthetic consumption and in political activism. We witnessed, for instance, the incredible rise of the Beatles and the ensueing 'pop scene', laughing the Establishment in the face. It was also a time of all kinds of rather planless civil disobedience. Significantly though, both reactions remained rather emotional, and generally yielded few political fruits.

Boredom and shocks

At this point, the question must once more be raised of how, in such a situation, human behaviour can still be stimulated at all. Human beings have only a very few, ill co-ordinated instincts that drive them; their thoughts, emotions and actions depend almost exclusively on meaningful interactions and traditional institutions, if it comes to behavioural stimulation. Thrown back on their own subjectivity, their organisms will not be able to send out sufficient

83

stimulation, since they are not self-reloading batteries. Hence, for his creativity, his mind, his sense of meaning and freedom, the individual depends almost exclusively on his fellow human beings with whom he should be able to interact meaningfully, as well as on traditional institutions which contain the values, norms and meanings that may guide him. However, when these grow abrstact, they can no longer assume this stimulating function.

It can be observed that speech becomes gross and hyperbolic, music loud and nervous, ideas giddy and fantastic, emotions limitless and shameless, actions bizarre and foolish, whenever boredom reigns. A bored individual needs these irritants of body, psyche and mind because he is not behaviourally stimulated in any other way. These irritants become collective movements in modern society, because of the search for news by the mass media and especially because of commercialization. As to the latter, when organized and presented in the right way (marketing), one can easily enlarge each faddish irritant into a very profitable mass 'hysteria': the drugs, the records, the books, the clothes – all are eagerly bought as long as they provide the wanted 'kicks'. In short, these shocks, loudly and hyperbolically advertised in cliché-ridden slogans, seem to be the substitutes for the lost stimulation formerly provided by the traditional institutions and their related, meaningful interactions.

The most striking examples of such collective shocks in modern abstract society are political revolts and revolutions. Many individuals seem to join a revolutionary movement not because they are strongly attracted by its programme but because of its tedium breaking shock-value – and it is these individuals who will eagerly engage in what Lenin once called 'infantile disorder'.

This rather unpolitical function of political revolts and revolutions is, in my opinion, very important. Ever since the onslaught of modernity, revolts against a *status quo* were not solely (and perhaps not even primarily) staged and propagated by economically uuderprivileged and politically repressed classes, but by the bored members of the well-to-do and ruling class. Anton Chekov, the great Russian playwright, described it very well in his *Three Sisters* which gives a magnificent picture of the combined boredom, anxiety, disgust and desire of the Russian upper-middle class prior to the revolution of 1917. One of the characters, Baron Tusenbach, remarks:[7]

'The yearning for work, oh dear, how well I understand it!
I have never worked in my life. . . . I was guarded from work.
But I doubt if they have succeeded in guarding me completely,
I doubt it! The time is at hand, an avalanche is moving down
upon us, a mighty clearing storm which is coming, is already
near and will soon blow the laziness, the indifference, the

distaste for work, the rotten boredom out of our society. I shall work, and in another twenty-five or thirty years every one will have to work. Every one!'

In the 1960s we witnessed the same sentiment. Ideologies of rebellion and revolt produced considerable excitement: at times they created partial and temporary chaos, as in numerous universities in the West. They sent temporary shock-waves through abstract society, extensively recorded and widely relayed through the media. But precisely who Mario Savio or Cohn-Bendit were has been forgotten within ten years. Excitement was caught in rhetoric, and rhetoric lead to boredom. 'We really felt we were going to overthrow the government in two or three years', one of the student leaders of the 1960s recently said in an interview. 'We had a sense of importance that would have led us to risk our lives for our rhetoric. By the end everybody had a label – pig, liberal, radical, revolutionary – and you had a few key questions to find out what their label was.'[8]

These irritation-provoking shocks can be found in all sectors of modern society. But the more often they are being sent out, the more they will lose their stimulating power, the more they will yield only cliché thoughts and emotions. To give just one example, I quote from a recent newspaper critique covering the appearance of a young violinist who left 'classical' music and became an expert in pop-music. Even fans must read such a hyperbolic piece of writing with amused boredom:[9]

> P. is a player skilled enough to use the violin to communicate directly with the listener, massaging his entire nervous system and re-arranging the sensibilities with multi-layered waves of orchestrated sound. . . . The fine music was marred by a sound system cranked up so far it left thousands of ears ringing in the cavernous hall.

Meanwhile, if he will not soon be marketed and widely distributed by a record company, violinist P. will be delivered to oblivion, irrespective of his talents. We can now better understand the intrinsic relationship between such boredom and clichés.

Boredom and rhetoric

Ideas, notions and theories which, for the lack of institutional stimulation, function as ideological stimulants of emotions, will become rhetoric in nature. A bored individual who embraces an ideology for the tedium-breaking excitement it has to offer, is of course not much interested in its precise theoretical meaning. Many radical students in the 1960s embraced Marxism without having any knowledge of the writings of Marx or Engels. *Das Kapital* by

Marx was probably the most bought and least read book of this century – incidentally, not the only feature it shares with the Bible. When called upon to legitimate theoretically their radical behaviour, these self-appointed Marxists would resort to a rambling account of the basic theorems of historical materialism – such clichés as 'infrastructure/superstructure', 'the unity of theory and praxis', 'the dialectical method', 'the emancipation of the underprivileged', etc. Even their theoretically somewhat better informed intellectual leaders would barely transcend the level of cliché discourse. Histomat (the abbreviated cliché that stands for 'Historical Materialism'), as used by them in lectures and speeches, was rarely more than a cliché-ridden rhetoric.[10]

Rhetoric is primarily the technique of using language effectively. Ideological rhetoric tries to stimulate individuals to think, feel and act in a way which coincides with the political goal of the group that espoused the ideology initially. At the same time, this rhetoric functions as a legitimation of this political goal and of the political behaviour that tries to realize this goal.

However, most important is the fact that ideological rhetoric contains moral norms and value-judgments which are in no way carried by stable conviction, but espoused and used by force of convention. As a result, participation in a rhetoric-ridden political movement is quite unreliable. The participants may suddenly get bored or even disgusted with the clichés of the ideology and drop from sight. It is clearly not enough to excite people with such slogans as 'power to the people' and 'power from the barrel of a gun'. In order to keep such a movement together, one needs the totalitarian control of a party. But then, one thing is certain, romantic Gnostics in search of emotional shocks are usually unable to bear the totalitarian control of party discipline. They want no discipline; they want experience, feeling, emotion.

There is, however, still another technique for keeping members under the wings of a rhetorical ideology. When its clichés have become boring, they can regain their stimulating effect by means of sheer, planless activism. In such a case, movements often resort to bizarre, if not violent behaviour. Quite often, this behaviour is no longer even legitimated by ideological clichés: it is a plain and simple *vivere pericolosamente*.

Beyond boredom and clichés

As I said earlier, Baudelaire knew *ennui* better than anyone else around him and once said, not without trepidation, that a bored individual is dangerous, because he would be perfectly willing to destroy the whole world. We now know the cause of this aggression and violence: the search of the bored for emotional shocks and irrational 'kicks' (either aesthetic or political) which is doomed to end in frustration. This frustration in turn is doomed to end either in dull resignation (sometimes of a psycho-pathological nature), or in meaningless and bizarre deeds.[11]

Not being instinctive automatons, people cannot live for long on semantically empty formulas. The rhetorical clichés will sooner or later lose their emotional shock value. In such a situation, only deeds can bring about new 'life', new 'aura', new 'charisma'. However, recent history has taught us that this kind of *vivere pericolosamente* may cause excitement, but it does not at all create humane aura and charisma. On the contrary, it has created in Italian and German fascism an historically almost incomparable life-destroying tyranny, whose aura and charisma were partly preposterous (cf. Mussolini) and partly demonic (cf. Hitler).[12] We should not disregard this historical lesson by labelling fascism 'right' and 'reactionary', while professing to be 'left' and 'progressive'. Bizarre deeds – whether performed in the name of fascism or in the name of Communism, or in the name of any other ideology – no longer relate to ideological values and norms. They will be performed under the flag of any set of clichés. As Pareto observed, the derivations are irrelevant, it is the residues that drive people impulsively. Pareto was certainly wrong when he used this as a generally valid model of human behaviour. The model is, however, very much applicable to the functions of ideological clichés.

Since the late 1960s, the world has time and again witnessed bizarre and often extremely aggressive acts, performed in the name of lofty, highly rhetorical ideologies. In almost all cases it was very hard to see how these utterly cruel acts of terrorism did in effect contribute anything to the realization of the political cause for which these ideologies allegedly stood. Someone, obviously with the knowledge of experience, once described terrorist acts such as those in Ireland, those of the German '*Rote Armee Fraktion*', of the Japanese 'Red Army', or the Italian 'Red Brigade', as 'mushrooms growing on a corpse' – the corpse, I should like to add, being *not* capitalist society, but the abstract ideology in the name of which human beings are being held in captivity and often murdered. All terrorism seems to offer is a *vivere pericolosamente* for the terrorists as well as for their captive victims. Meanwhile, the *kamikaze* behaviour of these terrorists lacks any trace of sense or honour.

It seems as if, beyond the supersedure of meaning by function, beyond clichés and boredom, lies the realm of the bizarre, the absurd, but also of the aggressive and of the cruel. It does indeed constitute the end of boredom and the end of the tyranny of the cliché; but then, it constitutes the end of anything that is human too.

87

5 Clichés bound

Stratagems to relativize the power of clichés

Introduction

Clichés are essential to communication. The Gnostic dream of the total abolition of clichés in social life, bringing about a 'pure' existence without the alienation of routinized and worn-out meanings, has in the end always led to a powerful dictatorship of the cliché. Perhaps more than anyone else, the Gnostic is caught in the web of his clichés. Likewise, Gnostic anti-institutionalism may easily engender repression of human beings 'in the name of freedom'. In this respect, the fate of Marxism, Existentialism and Freudianism is quite illuminating. Despite the admittedly wide range of differences between the three, these movements of thought and action share a strong Gnostic thrust. Not surprisingly, most of modern man's philosophical and political clichés have been coined in their orbits. Yet, the adepts and epigones of these movements, including the savants who adhere to one or the other mixture of them (cf. French Structuralism, or German 'critical theory' – the so-called '*Frankfurter Schule*') have never effectively promoted human creativity and freedom. They simply produced innumerable words, as well as innumerable clichés. Their initially renovating ideas grew inescapably into rather worn-out ideologies, couched in jargon and repeated like sacred mantras by intellectuals and semi-intellectuals. It was hoped, apparently, that such repetition might mobilize people and legitimate certain acts and life-styles.

The state of Marxism in Russia and China is, in this respect, quite significant. As has been demonstrated clearly by developments in Russia, Marxist practice routinized into a massive bureaucracy, while its theoretical system degenerated into a worn-out ideology stuffed with hackneyed phrases and cliché ideas. Any attempt to resist this abstract system of clichés in the name of socialism or humanism (as did dissidents from Sacharov to Solzhenitsyn) are, understandably, rather vehemently repressed. For if an ideology has lost its substantive rationality, it has to cling with all means available to its remaining functional rationality.

The current of events in China, meanwhile, has demonstrated clearly that the policy of a permanent Cultural Revolution which is supposed to shake up the bureaucratic colossus at regular intervals pumping socialist charisma into the masses again, may bring lots of excitement and commotion, but drives the country simultaneously to the brink of economic chaos and social anarchy. Since the rehabilitation of the pragmatic Teng, Mao's 'Little Red Book' will simply function as a dusty compilation of ideological mantras – clichés that children should learn by heart, and that adults repeat endlessly as a token of their ideologically correct spirit and mentality. In no way will this result in an ideological liberalization. On the contrary, when an ideology has become indispensable for the legitimation of existing political power structures, its worn-out clichés will be defended fiercely by the vehement repression of any attempt to deviate from them.

The word 'democracy', Fowler's 'Humpty-Dumpty word' of modernity, has become a worn-out cliché. Yet, for lack of a better term, I venture to say that one of the marks of a truly democratic society consists in the fact that it dares to consciously resist political clichés and that it allows its citizens to search for new political meanings beyond and outside the reign of the existing ideological clichés. When a worn-out ideology is repressively maintained in the name of sheer functional rationality, democracy has collapsed.

This chapter discusses the question of how the power of clichés in modern society can be bound, restricted, limited. We shall try to avoid the trap that awaits any headstrong confrontation with clichés; we shall maintain that clichés are as indispensable to human language and behaviour as the institutions. But we shall also maintain that stratagems can and have been developed which enable us to restrict and limit the tyranny of clichés. The anthropologically essential balance between meaning and function can be consciously maintained and, if need be, restored.

Prophetic-religious movements

It we take a bird's eye view of the long and complicated history of religion, we see an intrinsic though strained bond between religion and magic. This was discussed briefly earlier, but must be taken up once more in the present context.

Religion may be, idealtypically, described as the provider of meanings. In their religion, human beings view themselves, animals, objects and events – in short, the world, or reality – as a meaningful configuration. Religion develops a world-view which has primarily a heuristic function: it explains questions of meaning (which will arise in the face of suffering, destruction and death) and it legitimates behaviour. Religion has functionaries (specialists) who teach, interpret, maintain or adjust the world-view. They are frequently members of a specific school of thought with its specific hermeneutic tradition, and in almost all cases these functionaries belong to a societal élite as part of a powerful organization (hierocracy of a church). Max Weber has viewed religions – in particular those belonging to the type of religion-of-redemption – as the historical sources of rationalization.

Magic, on the other hand, can be, idealtypically, described as the provider of techniques by which individuals may manipulate alleged spiritual power (*mana*) to their own advantage. Usually, magicians do not engage in heuristic activities (explanation of reality, interpretation of a world-view, etc.) and consequently do not belong to specific schools of thought. They are professionals who are specialized in the manipulation of *mana*. If they are at all organized, they belong to gild-like groups. Moreover, they do not address themselves with sacred, theoretical knowledge to the community as a whole, as do priests and prophets. They rather train individuals who in their early years already demonstrated a gift for magic, some 'magical musicality'. Consequently Max Weber viewed magic as a force which runs counter to rationalization. (I criticized this view in chapter 1, stating that both religion and magic represent forms of rationality: the former is more substantially, the latter more functionally rational.) It must be stressed once more that such distinctions are idealtypical. That is, in the empirical reality of the history of religion, the two cannot at all be distinguished. In all the world religions, religious rituals and their connected cognitions and emotions have been penetrated by magic. In fact, only the prophets of ancient Judaism and Weber's 'religious virtuosos' of early Calvinism came near to the pure type of a radically anti-magical religion. But by separating the two idealtypically, we may grasp the anti-magical potential and thus the anti-cliché thrust of religious movements. This needs further qualification.

Magic is based on the notion that repetition engenders power. The formulas have to be repeated over and over again (cf. the mantras of Hinduism). Their wording and the accompanying gestures may not be altered. Acts and words are strictly structured according to formalistic and very ancient schemes. It is, moreover, neither the semantic content of the words and sentences, nor the meaning of these gestures that will activate *mana*, but it is the repetitive cadence which allegedly compels *mana* to emerge. In magic we encounter thus utterly cliché-ridden speech and behaviour. There is no room for creativity and ingenuity, for inventive play and variation. The movements of body and mind are caught in a very strict choreography. They follow ancient grooves that have little semantic content, but are believed to be very functional. In all this, magic resembles very much the functionality of clichés. In fact, nowhere is the tyranny of clichés stronger than in cultures predominated by magic.

When magic heavily penetrates religion, the latter's world-view and rituals will inevitably embrace this notion of necessary repetition: its tradition grows stale and spiritually repressive (cf. scholasticism). Yet, religion is potentially an anti-magical force. As Weber demonstrated in his essays on the sociology of religion, religions-of-redemption (*Erlösungsreligionen*) of the prophetic type – foremost ancient prophetic Judaism and Puritanism – will openly and almost aggressively attack magic. The prophets will debunk the certainty and security that magic promises. Magic, they will maintain, is false, treacherous and man-made. Prophetic faith is the result of Revelation, magic is just human projection.

Morally, the prophetic religion will oppose magical determinism and fatalism by stressing man's responsibility *vis-à-vis* God and the world. It sets against the routines of magical behaviour, man's duty to realize his potential. Moreover, it explains reality in terms that often shatter the taken-for-granted routines of daily life. The prophetic message is never a comfortable one: it entials a 'precarious vision'[1] without clichés to lean on. Measured by the norms of commonsense, prophets were usually extra-ordinary, if not plainly mad.

Inevitably, the prophetic movement of ancient Judaism (mainly under the impact of the Exile) routinized into the rabbinical tradition, while the prophetic movement of the Reformation (mainly under the impact of capitalism) routinized into the secularized Protestant ethic. Clichés took over again, while charisma grew stale. Yet, for the duration of their influence, they have managed to break the tight web of magical clichés, thus demonstrating that clichés are not metaphysically tied to the human condition, that they do not constitute the eternal and immovable limits of human existence. When and where this is deemed necessary, the tyranny of clichés can apparently be broken – even if eventually the charisma that brought this about, is doomed to routinize again and engender its own clichés.

It is, of course, highly questionable if such prophetic–religious movements could ever again gain the social and political prominence which they acquired in pre-modern society. Sociologically speaking, a Jeremiah or Muhammed, a Jesus or Calvin could in abstract and pluralistic society only arouse religious excitement in a small portion of the mass of the population. The charisma of their message would in no way be rejected, because rejection would still imply that their message was taken seriously. On the contrary, it would be looked upon as 'something quite interesting'; it would be broadcast, televized and commercialized as a curiosity, as would happen to all the counter-prophecies that would emerge immediately as competition in its wake. Meanwhile, modern religious revivalism has long since surrendered to Madison Avenue, which teaches it how to wrap up its message in the clichés of a comfortable, religious kitsch. These messages may well yield considerable economic profits, but they are hardly prophetic. It is a far cry from Billy Graham to Jeremiah, not so much in time as in spirit and mentality; between them lie in particular many, many clichés.

Scientific discoveries

The modern world has, in a sense, substituted science for prophetic religion. This should not be read in a scientistic sense. Scientism is the ideological belief, first formulated by the Enlightenment and repeated up to the present day, that the religious 'truths' of the unenlightened past have been unmasked as childish superstitions by the Truth of Rationalism and Science. Scientism is, furthermore, founded on the belief that science will enable man to know reality objectively and in exact (mathematically precise) terms, while religious knowledge of reality will remain subjective, metaphysical and generally mythological. Finally, scientism is the belief that science can bring about 'progress for all', while religion keeps people tied to the past and to the powerful *status quo* of traditional and outdated institutions. In sum, scientism is a rather dated ideology with a very stale, cliché set of prejudices. It was very vigorous in Darwinism, Marxism, and Freudianism, and it still haunts those social sciences that are firmly and comfortably couched in neo-positivism.

In this context I mean to follow Weber who viewed science as a rather unintended consequence of the rationalization caused by prophetic religions-of-redemption. (His argument as to the elective affinity between Puritan ethics and the spirit of capitalism can easily be applied to the relation between the former and modern science. This has been done by R. K. Merton.)[2] Although science can never compete with the heuristic and redeeming function of these religions – it cannot answer questions as to the meaning of life and death, suffering and pain, joy and happiness – it yet has the intention of explaining and interpreting reality as an ordered and thus understandable configuration. In this sense, there is definitely a continuum between religion and science.

The continuum is very apparent in the late Middle Ages and the Renaissance. The first great scientific discoverers (Copernicus, Bruno, Kepler, Galileo, etc.) ran into a conflict with the Roman Church over some 'natural-scientific' (Aristotelean and Ptolemean) tenets, but did not generally question the religious doctrines of the Church. Bertolt Brecht's famous play *Leben des Galilei*, depicting this scientist as a rebel against the Church and against Christianity, tells us more about Brecht's own, Marxist scientism than about Galileo's religious beliefs and unbeliefs.

In medieval Scholasticişm the idea had already been developed that reality could be studied *'etsi Deus non daretur'* ('as if God does not exist'). To these, mainly nominalistic theologians God did 'of course' exist, but they found it worthwhile to look at reality and study it by bracketing His existence.

Following Whitehead, G. H. Mead drew our attention to still another element of this continuum between religion and science.[3] The natural sciences have always been guided by the idea that reality is lawfully structured. These sciences should reconstruct the laws of nature and formulate them as precisely as possible (mathematics). This is precluded by the religious notion that the world was created by God according to a plan and that man could acquire (theological) knowledge of this plan and of the structured order it has created. In fact, for a very long time scientists believed they were actually reconstructing God's creative work by discovering and interpreting the fundamental laws of nature.

The scientific discoveries of Copernicus, Kepler, Bruno, Galileo and others thus shocked those elements of the late-medieval religious world-view which were not so much religious as 'natural scientific'. These were mainly some Aristotelean and Ptolemean tenets which, in medieval Scholasticism, had received magical status. In his play on Galileo Brecht shows us a medieval Scholastic who refuses to look through a telescope. Afterall, he knows 'his' Aristotelean philosophy and Ptolemean cosmology, what conceivably could he learn from looking through that thing? Others, however, did and it eventually reduced the 'natural scientific' elements of the Aristotelean and Ptolemean world-view to smithereens: its clichés were radically shattered.

Naturally, these discoveries and the world-view that emerged in their wake, became routinized in their turn. They eventually and necessarily also developed a rather strict frame of reference, spelling out how to look at the world, how to examine it, how to formulate it theoretically. They became a paradigm which spelt out the real problems and how they could possibly be solved – science as the solving of puzzles (Kuhn).[4] Thus, clichés ruled again. Only a revolutionary, new set of discoveries, such as those of Bohr, Einstein,

93

Oppenheimer, etc. which showed scientists how to look differently at reality, how to ask different questions and how to come up with different answers, could smash the cliché of the Copernican world-view.[5]

Understandably, many scientists, comfortably installed in the clichés of a worn-out paradigm (in the mastering of which they had invested quite some cognitive and emotive energies), will hesitate to accept the new paradigm. They will sometimes ridicule its proponents, perhaps blocking their further career. This is precisely what happened to Freud in Vienna.[6] But when the discoveries are eventually accepted, they may well develop into another paradigm with its mantra-like tenets and ready-made clichés. Once more, Freud's psycho-analytic movement presents a good example.[7]

Paradigms can obtain the vast range and scope of a world-view (Aristotelean, Copernican, Einsteinean physics; Marxism, Darwinism, Freudianism), influencing scientists far outside their own specific discipline (cf. Social Darwinism). They can also remain limited to one discipline (cf. Structural Functionalism in sociology) and even within this discipline occur in a competing plurality. The latter is obviously the case with the sociological discipline which knows several mutually competing paradigms. After the Second World War, sociology was (for sociologically quite understandable reasons) dominated by the neo-positivistic paradigm. During the 1960s other paradigms began to compete with it, notably the neo-Marxist and phenomenologically oriented approaches to social reality (cf. 'new-left sociology', 'critical theory', 'symbolic interactionism', 'ethnomethodology'). Much of the alleged crisis of this discipline is caused by the fact that by now the clichés of these competing paradigms have become routinized, common property, while their points of mutual disagreement are also rather well known. That is, they no longer provide material for intellectually stimulating debates. This stalemate becomes quite clear, if one leafs through the pages of various sociological journals. Likewise, most sociological congresses and conferences remind the observer of magical rituals in which clichés are repeated over and over again.

To sum up, scientific discoveries may indeed break the tyranny of clichés, but like the religious movements, they are doomed eventually to routinize and develop paradigms in which clichés will rule again. Nevertheless, like the prophetic movements discussed previously, such scientific discoveries at least demonstrate that the tyranny of clichés can be broken, even if the collapse of their reign is only temporary. Such breaches of cliché power relativize it and show us that we can obstruct its eternal prolongation. An absolute, definitive and total victory is impossible, yet we can constantly try to shift the limits which clichés impose on our language and behaviour.

This is, probably, the most essential characteristic of human culture.

Meanwhile, as the history of science clearly demonstrates, scientific man too has always been lured by the Gnostic dream of a total and definitive victory over the power of clichés. Ever since Copernicus, who dramatically changed the medieval world-view, scientists have consciously searched for a radical and fundamental overhaul of the theories and methods of their discipline. In philosophy, for example, Kant believed and in fact said that his epistemology presented a Copernican change in philosophy. Durkheim believed that his discovery of the 'social facts' was a Copernican change within the Copernican change of Kant: the categories of Kant's epistemology, he claimed, were not at all transcendental and *a priori*, but socio-cultural and historical, namely 'social facts'. Husserl too viewed his phenomenological method as a Copernican change, overthrowing radically the Cartesian subject–object dualism. And Marx performed quite consciously a Copernican change by 'putting Hegel on his feet'.

These were indeed 'paradigmatic revolutions' (Kuhn) which must have exhilirated their inventors and early followers. It has, however, rarely been noted that they gave rise to a special phenomenon which I would like to call the 'Copernican Change Syndrome'. By this I mean the rather Gnostic desire on the part of individual scientists and philosophers also to make a revolutionary contribution to their field of scientific or philosophical research, for once to secure for themselves a place in the scientific 'hall of fame', and to be thus immortalized alongside the 'great' and 'classic' names in the field. As a result, a scientist who has some success in his field of research is liable to view himself and to be viewed by others (publishers in the first place) as a potential 'classic'. Frequently he begins to act like a *prima donna* or Hollywood star – social roles transferred from show business to science in order to boost, not the scientific discipline, but the scientist's ego.[8]

As a result, such Gnostic dreamers who engage in scientific work primarily for the sake of self-aggrandizement (very much like the previously discussed young pianists taken to task by Arturo Michelangeli), and who consequently cannot see themselves as servants of science, will in almost all cases end up frustrated and hence become unbearable to their friends, relatives and colleagues. If, as I intimated at the very start of this study, a paradigmatic revolution would no longer be objectively possible in a discipline like sociology, the Gnostic dream of a Copernican change is going to cause utter frustration. Much talk about an already existing or an allegedly still coming crisis for sociology originates precisely in this very frustration.

Commercialization is bound to reinforce this syndrome. In order to boost sales, publishers often start an advertising campaign praising a particular book with such clichés as 'a classic in the field' or 'a definitive study', while its authors are compared to the greatest names in the history of the sciences. Bishop Robinson, the author of a pleasant little book, *Honest to God*, which caused much excitement within and outside theology in the first half of the 1960s, was heralded as a 'theological Galileo' and a 'theological Freud'. Ten years later, however, nobody could even remember his name – including many of those who had read the book. The same happened to Marcuse, McLuhan, Laing, *et tutti quanti*. In fact, they did not bring any scientific renewal at all. They manufactured or revived clichés – in some cases of a clearly Gnostic nature – were received with enthusiasm, consumed, were barely digested than they were disposed of again. One fact, however, remains: they were commercially very attractive. If manipulated shrewdly, the 'Copernican Change Syndrome' can indeed yield considerable commercial profit.

Thus, the Gnostic, headstrong attack on clichés in science is not a very adequate strategem. It may, on the contrary, very well enhance their power, as in an unintended consequence. Scientific renewal and its inherent transcendence of clichés will, nowadays, probably only be possible in a gradual and piecemeal fashion. Constantly aware of their power, the scientist and the philosopher should carefully try to shift and stretch the limits which clichés impose on their thought and research. As to the social sciences, it is not likely that a Copernican change, as a spectacular collapse of an entire system of clichés, is at all feasible now or in the future – not least because these clichés hardly constitute a system! But even if such a paradigmatic revolt were at all possible, the individual social scientist should not constantly search and yearn for it. The history of the sciences has shown anyway that the most radical renewals were by no means consciously sought for and planned, just as the history of religions has demonstrated that the really great prophets were never self-appointed. This is the dimension of calling and of anti-Gnostic, intellectual asceticism[9]: it constitutes the essence of what Weber called 'science as a vocation'. A scientific discipline becomes an intellectually dreadful place to dwell when it has lost this dimension. All kinds of competing theoretical fads, lauded commercially as 'truly revolutionary' changes and improvements in the field, may at regular intervals cause confusion and excitement, but they will lack all aura and eventually produce only boredom.

Socio-political movements

Most socio-political movements do not merely focus on political and legal changes of the *status quo* in a society, but also aim at a change of mentality and ethos. In doing so, they have to confront deep-seated clichés, generally taken for granted which in daily parlance and in the social sciences are called prejudices. The Civil Rights Movement of the late 1950s and early 1960s in the USA and the various action groups of the Feminist Movement of the late 1960s and 1970s are very clear examples. Usually, such socio-political movements are initially driven by a few charismatic and highly inventive individuals who try to mobilize people for their cause and to debunk systematically the generally accepted clichés which run counter to this cause. They will, above all, try to convince people that a certain state of affairs in society is not just immoral and illegitimate, but also illegal and unconstitutional, arguing in terms of natural and constitutional law and of the Geneva Convention, if need be. When they criticize the immoral and illegitimate dimensions of this state of affairs, they will focus their attack on the prejudices which morally support it.

Obviously, the Civil Rights Movements managed to bring about some legal adjustments and to shatter some racist clichés with regard to the position of blacks in American society. The cliché stance 'they should know their place' should certainly not be evident anymore. Likewise, the impact of feminism has somewhat improved the legal and socio-economic position of women in modern society and has at least made us aware of certain male prejudices which were, until recently, usually taken for granted. Nor can the cliché 'the woman's place is in the home' be used any longer without any reservation or reflection.

However, as in prophetic–religious movements and scientific discoveries, the initial charisma of such socio-political movements is doomed eventually to routinize once more. An important factor is the fact that they have to mobilize people who are generally quite passive and uncommitted, due to the nature of modern, abstract society. The values which are being launched on the offensive against the existing prejudices will necessarily be of free-floating character and so weak. As a result, socio-political movements will increasingly try to shock people and to mobilize them behaviouristically with the help of clichégenic slogans. That is, their message turns into propaganda.

When a socio-political movement has reached this stage, we have a situation in which prejudices are no longer confronted by a deviating point of view and by deviating values. It is a situation in which clichés are at war with clichés. Still, significant socio-economic and legal victories may be won in this war. These are, however, victories in terms of political power, not moral victories over the tyranny of clichés.

Generally, therefore, socio-political movements are only able to design inventive stratagems against cliché power in their initial phase. Politically, they may not yet be very strong in this phase, but

97

morally, in terms of a human attack on the tyranny of clichés in society, this stage may well be the most vigorous and powerful.

Aesthetic sublimation

When clichés rule the field of art, literature and music, we speak of *kitsch*, a term that is extremely difficult to define.[10] But we can list a few dominant characteristics. First, the products of kitsch are, so to speak, easy to consume and easy to digest: kitsch caters for existing tastes. Aesthetic renewal and originality are not its aim, and it is not founded on any sophisticated aesthetic ideas or theories. As the producer of kitsch purposefully caters to existing tastes, and wants to satisfy existing consumer needs with ease, he will apply worn-out techniques and worn-out themes, which in turn: appeal to worn-out emotions.

A second characteristic follows on from this. In kitsch everything is harmonious and unproblematic: controversies and conflicts are at all times avoided. The producer of kitsch will never venture into any experiments which might unintentionally cause disagreement and friction. He certainly does not aspire to the controversial or to frustrate potential customers. But not only will his painting, sculpting and writing techniques remain conventional, his substantive themes will also consciously avoid any matter which is possibly controversial. In the novels of Hedwig Courts-Mahler, for instance, the *dramatis personae* (and dramatic they certainly are), are being driven continuously by compassion and love. Nature is at all times radiant and in harmony with the course of events – which, of course, is always a tragic course, although at the end of each novel the tragedy always alters for the better. Naturally, too, the protagonists inhabit the best of all possible worlds: they belong to the nobility or upper-bourgeoisie, dwell in castles, and are surrounded by faithful servants and hard working, happy peasants. Sometimes people are angry, but their anger is always just and justified. They are never nasty, ugly or spiteful – unless they are the scoundrels and culprits who at the end receive their just deserts.

A third characteristic of kitsch lies in the fact that it appeals to emotions which we tend to call 'cheap'. That is, kitsch tries to avoid any form of cognition or reflection; it wants to touch the consumer emotionally only. In the paintings of religious kitsch, Jesus is 'sweet' and 'radiant' and so beautiful that one would literally like to embrace him. In a novel by Courts-Mahler, the count is so noble and the tragedy he has to cope with so tragic, that one cannot but love him deeply and passionately sympathize with him. The effect kitsch wants to bring about is unproblematic empathy and sympathy on the part of the consumer.

Fourth, cognitive reflections have to be avoided because they are lethal to kitsch. If one steps back and reflects upon kitsch, it becomes literally ridiculous, and so loses its effect. Kitsch calls for feeling, not thought. Consequently, kitsch generally appeals to those social classes and categories that do not rely heavily on reflection in daily social life: lower-middle and working classes, and the non-working women of the upper and middle classes (cf. novels such as those of Pearl Buck serialized in women's magazines).

The intelligentsia – academics, artists, writers, journalists – has in general a two-fold relationship to kitsch: it often furnishes its designers and producers, and at certain times members of the intelligentsia may themselves also consume and enjoy kitsch. These are the times at which they deliberately try to exclude cognitive reflections (cf. vacations). There is, however, a further way in which members of the intelligentsia may relate to kitsch and its clichés: they can consciously and deliberately produce and consume kitsch as a kind of *aesthetic sublimation*. Kitsch is, then, defined as being 'actually quite funny' and 'actually quite nice', or it is accepted in terms of 'what is good for the masses, is good enough for the intelligentsia' – an obviously ideological, anti-intellectualist position. This is still the consumption aspect of aesthetic sublimation; the production side is more relevant to the main issue of the present chapter.

Kitsch has been deliberately produced in a sublimated manner by artists and writers who have tried to provide political criticism and expose the *status quo* of bourgeois society and culture. In Dadaism, for example, the use of kitsch clichés has been a common technique in the game of *épater le bourgeois*. In many of Bertolt Brecht's plays, elements of kitsch – cliché ideas and emotions – occur which were meant in a politically critical manner. By using them cynically, Brecht hoped to rouse his bourgeois audience to reflection – reflection which would alienate them from their bourgeois values, norms and meanings.

Whether one can accept the tenets of Dadaist anarchism or Brechtian Marxism or not, these aesthetic sublimations do represent a temporary victory over the power of clichés. Here they are deliberately used and abused, twisted and overturned. The politician and the missionary will also manipulate clichés, but they remain generally tied to them as an ideological conviction. They will, moreover, try to tie others to these clichés in a political or religious conversion. Brecht and the Dadaists, on the contrary, used the clichés of bourgeois society cynically in order to shatter them. The music and text of the *Threepenny Opera* by Kurt Weill and Bertolt Brecht, for instance, is full of bourgeois clichés. On a superficial hearing, it all sounds like kitsch, but if one pays closer attention –

and by means of so-called 'alienating effects' (*Verfremdungseffekte*) Weill and Brecht make us reflect upon these songs – one suddenly realizes that bourgeois society and its favourite clichés is being cynically ridiculed and severely taken to task. The political effect of Brecht's 'epic theatre' on bourgeois and capitalist society is probably nil. Certainly, the anti-bourgeois songs of the *Threepenny Opera* have missed their target. Ever since its premiere (1928), these songs have been stock material of the musical kitsch of modern society, called *muzak*. 'Mack the Knife' is heared in supermarkets and airports, in restaurants and at the barber's – kitsch to be easily consumed and digested.

Thus, Brecht and the Dadaists indeed managed, at least temporarily, to subject kitsch and its clichés to their creative and often inventive power. But eventually, this victory too was again overtaken by routinization and the tyranny of clichés. Today, the products of the Dadaists are exhibited in museums of modern art, and the plays of Bertolt Brecht are consumed and digested by theatre goers who admire his creativity, but are not at all convinced by the Marxist message which he was trying to convey. Indeed, snobism was the greatest enemy of these fighters against the tyranny of clichés.

(Brecht did 'believe' in Marxism and its ideological set of clichés. Yet, as is well known, while living in East Berlin his mental cast and life style, as well as a couple of his plays, caused some serious problems to the Party *apparatchiks*. For instance, he would offer guests Western whisky and Havanna (pre-Castro) cigars, and it has been claimed that he had a bank account in Switzerland. It appears as if his belief in Marxist clichés was infinitely less firm than his hatred of the values and norms of bourgeois society.)

The works of Brecht and the products of the Dadaists present Marxist and anarchist attacks on the clichés of bourgeois society. These, in fact, are *political* sublimations of kitsch in art and literature; there are also *purely aesthetic* sublimations of kitsch and its clichés. The music of Gustav Mahler is a good example.

Unlike Richard Strauss who tried to carry the classical and romantic tradition of the eighteenth and nineteenth centuries into the twentieth century, admittedly modifying it in order to render it suitable for modern ears, Gustav Mahler seems to have tried to end and transcend this tradition, thus paving the way for Arnold Schoenberg and Alban Berg, and beyond them for serial and electronic music, and so-called *musique concrète* (which, in fact, is more abstract than its name indicates). Mahler was a romantic who deliberately tried to end Romanticism, and one of the main techniques he used for the realization of this aim was the purely aesthetic sublimation of kitsch. Not only the technical instrumentation of his symphonies

100

and his song cycles (such as *Kindertotenlieder* and *Das Lied von der Erde*), but also the thematic material of the music and the texts are kitsch, consciously remoulded to art. His was not at all an anarchist or Marxist critique of bourgeois society and culture; on the contrary, Mahler was utterly bourgeois. He was an aesthete and post-romantic who realized that romantic emotions and experiences were doomed to be clichés in a modern, increasingly abstract society. He took them and consciously turned them into music. In a Mahler symphony the serious listener travels, as it were, through kitsch and arrives at a level which has transcended kitsch. Only when taken apart and separated from the rest of the symphony, does a single Mahler theme retain its cliché character and remain kitsch. Not surprisingly, films quite often use Mahler fragments in their music these days. (Much of film music is prone to kitsch since it facilitates unproblematic consumption.) But if taken as a totality, if listened to attentively from beginning to end, a Mahler symphony guides the listener through many clichés to a level of aesthetic experience which has transcended clichés. This indeed is a very rare example of a victory over the cliché. It is important to observe that Mahler did not launch a headstrong attack on clichés, but rather subdued them to his creative power by incorporating them into his work. He incorporated clichés, worked on them, remoulded them, and then elevated them beyond kitsch.[11]

Comic sublimation

I have described humour elsewhere as social play with traditional, institutionalized meanings.[12] Humour, which I use as a general concept to include such barely distinguishable phenomena as wit and comedy, is a social phenomenon. In order to joke and laugh, we need the company of at least one partner: it is very much a matter of social interaction. Second, in his humorous activities and exploits man is very much a *homo ludens*: in our humour, we play, we fool around, we leave the functional realm of daily routine and its chores, we enter a make-believe world in which in principle everything is possible. In humour, the values of social life are turned upside down, the norms of social hierarchies violated, the rules of language (grammar and syntax) and of logic suspended. We play with social roles, with our relation to authority, with gestures, with words and sentences, with logic. Third, the substance of humour, the material with which we play in humour, consists of traditional and institutionalized meanings: what had been taken for granted is put in a different perspective, what we always meant by 'left' is turned into 'right', what traditionally had been labelled 'bad' is changed to 'good' – wisdom changes into foolishness and the other way about,

101

while the two genders of the human species are interchanged. At least for the duration of the laughter elicited by jokes, the meanings that had been played with are relativized. Meanwhile, laughter turns out to be a very adequate response: it defines this play with institutionalized meanings as something not to be taken seriously; it communicates the fact that the legitimacy and plausibility of the meanings is not really affected, that reality still is what it has been before.

Not surprisingly, a favourite pastime in humour is playing with clichés. Professional humourists, from the medieval court jester to the modern comedian, have always played tricks on the clichés of daily routine. They often take a cliché, ridicule its original meaning, push it to absurd extremes, switch the original meaning or apply it in a totally different frame of reference. A whole range of humorous variations have been applied to such a cliché as 'a family that prays together stays together'. The conscious or unconscious transfer of a cliché from one frame of reference to a totally different one always manages to raise a laugh. A worn-out, hackneyed *zote*,[13] for example, coming out of the mouth of a nun, would highly surprise us and then strike us as 'very funny', although its meaning would no longer surprise us at all: it is like a swear-word transferred from the mouth of a soldier to the mouth of a member of the Salvation Army.

However, even this humorous play with clichés routinizes easily and thus gets deeply entangled in clichés. 'They all look alike' is a racist cliché, formerly applied quite often by Caucasians to Blacks and Orientals; today, television comedies quite often put these words in the mouths of Blacks and Orientals. This initially cliché-breaking technique, however, has by now lost its heuristic pith and became a humourless cliché. Even the laughter in such television comedies is cliché, and called – appropriately enough – 'canned laughter'. To use Mead's famous typology, the inventive *play* with meanings has turned into a routine *game* – that is, the manipulation of clichés in mirth has itself become a cliché, not in the least for commercial reasons. Also in the area of humour and laughter, commercialization has always been a strong clichégenic force.

Nevertheless, in our mirthful playing with traditional and routinized meanings – either as 'professionals' or, in everyday social life, as 'laymen' – we have a chance to subdue clichés to our ingenuity and wit, and thus to relativize their power. As in all the other stratagems discussed, the 'charisma' of humour is doomed to routinize and give way to the power of clichés. Yet, at least for the duration of the laughter it elicits, humour demonstrates that clichés are not invincible and not anthropologically 'essential'. Although for a short while, in much humour clichés are being bound, and the reign of their power is transcended.

102

Clichés and the stranger

Simmel has quite brilliantly pointed at the sociological dimensions of the stranger who, coming from the outside, enters the orbit of our norms, values motives and meanings, and begins to communicate with us. The social position of the stranger, I shall argue now, is sociologically quite significant as far as the reign of clichés is concerned.

First, the foreigner who begins to learn our culture and its language but who is not as yet well-versed in it, is liable to be pleasantly touched by our clichés. That is, not having been exposed yet to their repetitive use, a stranger can still enjoy the original ingenuity and wit of our clichés: meaning, to him, has not yet been superseded by function. Hackneyed English expressions like 'the fair sex', 'filthy lucre', 'in all walks of life', 'blessing in disguise' do not sound like clichés in his ears at all. They still strike him, on the contrary, as pretty, witty, acute, ingenious, etc. – just as they must have struck the native speakers of the language, when such expressions first came into use. Incidentally, the foreigner who launches into worn-out clichés and hackneyed thoughts with emphasis, a heavy accent and apparent conviction can be a source of great embarrassment or a cause for laughter, depending on the situation. He is, for example, embarrassing during a scientific congress, but quite hilarious in informal conversation, say during a party. Peter Sellers, the British master of cliché disguise, is a very skilled impersonator of such pathetically pompous foreigners.

Adolescents who are in the process of academic socialization (in the upper form of secondary school and college) also have the tendency to use intellectual clichés without much inhibitions and they are similarly quite prone to the aesthetic enjoyment of kitsch. Interesting in this respect is the so-called 'graduate-student-syndrome' in North-American universities: graduate students are generally rather ambitious and competitive individuals still in the process of learning and adopting the standard theorems and methods of their scientific discipline. In fact, these theorems and methods are still relatively new to them. They have to reproduce them during exams, and they are not yet able to play with them freely as in professional virtuosity. Meanwhile, to many of their teachers, these same theorems and methods are often not much more than clichés – much needed perhaps, yet eventually to be transcended.

Looked at more formally, this is the relationship between the dilettante and the professional. Since the former tends to quite humourlessly love what the latter masters professionally and, as it were, losely and smoothly, any social contact between the two is bound to give rise to mutual frustration. The professional gets easily

103

irritated by the dilettante's unskilled zeal and enthusiasm, the dilettante is disappointed by the professional's rather detached and *déjà vu* attitude. However, if they are both aware of this mechanism, they can profit greatly from one another. The professional could draw inspiration from the dilettante's enthusiasm and thus avoid the potential dreariness of his professionalism, while the dilettante could learn to professionally control his mostly irrational enthusiasm.

The sociological type of the stranger is, of course, not limited to the foreigner who has left his native country and thus entered from the outside into our society with its values, norms, motives and meanings. A stranger in the sociological sense is, in fact, every person who cannot or will not readily accept these norms, values, motives and meanings of ours: the child, the fool, the deviant, the criminal. If listened to, these sociological strangers – and in a pluralistic society there are many such – may confront us, as in a cultural confrontation, with our own clichés and they may coerce us in reflecting upon them. There have been societies in the past, in which strangers – from foreigners to fools – were treated as sacred, prophetic persons, not merely because they carried the aura of the unknown, but because they were allegedly able to make people aware again of the original and fundamental meanings of their daily social life – they had a hermeneutic function. By the contrast he presents, the stranger is able to momentarily suspend the supersedure of meaning by function and thus to relativize and limit the power of clichés.[14]

Conclusion

In this chapter I have selectively discussed various possible ways to relativize the tyrannic power of clichés. I have rejected the Gnostic search for a society and culture radically divested of any clichés, argueing that this search is unavoidably counter-productive – to use a rather hackneyed expression. It leads easily, though generally unintentionally, to a total victory for clichés. Instead, I have argued that clichés are indispensable to social life in general and to human communication in particular. Yet, there are historically specific, socio-cultural circumstances in which this functionality of clichés turns into a tyranny. Modern society was singled out as such a case. This led me to search for stratagems which could at least relativize and curb the tyrannical rule of clichés without falling for the lure of Gnosticism.

I do not pretend that this discussion of the various stratagems has been complete. I focused on the sectors of religion, politics, science, humour and aesthetics which, I believe, are and should be the main providers of such anti-cliché stratagems. A few examples were given in each case and the reader can undoubtedly add to these several more. Finally, I discussed the sociological position of the stranger as still another phenomenon which in principle has the power to relativize and limit the tyranny of clichés.

As to the clichés of modernity, we can – and in all sensibility, should – only aspire to keep a conscious check on their functionality. It is absolutely necessary for such an objective, rationally to undertsand this functionality and to continue to rationally search for stratagems which could relativize and curb it. I hope to have demonstrated that the sociological discipline, despite its sociologese, is still able to assist us in the realization of this goal.

Appendix

Cultural sociology and cultural analysis

If one compares present day sociology with the writings of such 'classics' as De Tocqueville, Weber, Durkheim, Simmel and Mannheim, one cannot fail to discover a set of differences which will lead one to conclude that there are, in fact, two kinds of sociology. One could, of course, characterize the efforts of these 'classics' as an early stage of the sociological discipline in which the foundations of our present 'modern' and 'more scientific' sociology were laid. Continuing the argument in this direction, one will view 'classic sociology' as a theoretically fruitful endeavour which, however, was at fault methodologically because it left too much room for speculation and failed to develop, first, adequate techniques for empirical research, and, second, concepts which could be operationalized quantitatively. As to the latter, Durkheim's concept of anomie is a notable exception, but Weber's notion of the capitalist 'Geist', Mannheim's leading idea of a 'Weltanschauungssystem' and Simmel's 'Formen der Vergesellschaftung' are obvious examples. To the 'modern' sociologist, such concepts are utterly irritating because of their alleged vagueness and lack of empirical precision. In this view of 'classic' sociology, one will perhaps read its main publications (De Tocqueville's book on American democracy, Durkheim's study on suicide, Weber's essay on Protestant ethics and the spirit of Capitalism, Mannheim's interpretation of ideology and Utopia, Simmel's theory of the web of group affiliations) as part of one's intellectual erudition which is anyhow rather scanty in 'modern' sociology. But when it comes to 'truly modern' empirical research, one may and easily will forget these allegedly vague and speculative theories. In short, 'modern' sociology is still the normative model today, and 'classic' sociology is only deemed relevant scientifically

106

if it somehow resembles this very model – as is, for example, the case with Durkheim's study on suicide which happened to make use of statistical data. As is well known, much time, energy and money has been spent by 'modern' sociologists in the construction of anomie-scales. Whether they were actually still speaking about that anomie which Durkheim worried so much about, is, of course, highly questionable. Likewise, the alienation-scales constructed by sociological operationalists have probably very little in common with the concept that Marx used in order to demonstrate the socio-psychological dimensions of the historical phenomenon of human exploitation.

It is my contention that one should view 'classic' and 'modern' sociology as two mutually complementary, but epistemologically and methodologically radically different approaches to socio-cultural reality. In this view, so-called 'classic' sociology is not an early, pre-scientific stage of 'modern' sociology, rather it stands on its own as an epistemologically and methodologically autonomous approach to socio-cultural reality. It has its own logical coherence and it adds dimensions to the sociological discipline which have been sorely lacking ever since the dominance of 'modern' sociology. Let us briefly (and thus inadequately) characterize both types of sociology.

For 'modern' sociology, we could list the following main features:
1   Although sociology originated in Europe, it has been a predominantly American affair ever since roughly the Second World War – i.e. 'modern' sociology is geared towards a fully modernized society invested with the values, norms, motives and meanings of modernity.
2   Epistemologically, this predominantly American sociology remains rooted in Anglo-Saxon empiricism, notably in the firm belief that truth consists of a correspondence between theory (concepts) and reality (facts). In particular, the alleged objectivity of the facts is at all times heavily emphasized.
3   Methodologically, this sociology is based on operationalism – i.e. it believes firmly that concepts should be made suitable to quantitative (statistical) research techniques. Consequently, all those concepts which cannot be operationalized quantitatively are doomed to remain 'philosophical', 'vague', 'speculative' – perhaps useful for the formulation of hypotheses, but in general irrelevant to empirical research.
4   The results of empirical research – the empirical theories about reality – should be verifiable and/or falsifiable by consecutive empirical research. The aim of research is – if not Truth – at least verisimilitude.
5   The research itself should be repeatable – i.e. other social

107

scientists must be able to engage in the very same piece of research by means of well-developed research techniques.

6 As a result of 3, 4 and 5 methodology has become increasingly the systematic construction and further development of research techniques. In fact, sociology has been identified more and more with the use of these techniques of empirical research.

7 Finally, this type of sociology believes that it should aspire to be pragmatic – i.e. it focuses predominantly on research which can be put to use in policy. Latently or manifestly, 'modern' sociology aspires to be policy oriented: sociology as an applied social science.

Apart from an Auguste Comte or Durkheim's study on suicide, 'classic' European sociology deviates from these features of 'modern' sociology rather radically. This is very obviously the case, when 'classic' sociologists make an effort to construct an epistemological and methodological foundation for their sociological observations and interpretations. This has been the case in particular in the neo-Kantian sociology of Weber and Simmel who both founded their sociological efforts on the epistemological writings of Heinrich Rickert. (This is, of course, not the place to discuss the many differences between Weber and Simmel, nor the differences between those two and Rickert.) In the sociology of Weber we encounter definitely a very specific approach to socio-cultural reality which deviates rather radically from 'modern' sociology. This is not an 'early' sociology which works with a necessarily still underdeveloped ('primitive') methodology. On the contrary, here we find a very specific approach with a specific epistemological and methodological foundation. It can be given different names. Weber himself called it 'verstehende Soziologie', usually translated as 'interpretive sociology' or 'interpretative sociology'. However, due to a fatal misinterpretation of the notion of Verstehen on the part of Anglo-Saxon empiricists, it is better to abandon this name for this type of sociology altogether. (Weber spoke of 'rational understanding' and did not view it as a method, as is usually believed in 'modern' sociology. The ideal types constitute the method, while rational Verstehen is viewed as the result of the application of the idealtypical method!)

Weber's sociology could be called a 'sociology of knowledge'. However, under the impact of 'modern' sociology one has come to view the sociology of knowledge no longer as a general approach, as it has been with Mannheim, Pareto and Scheler, but rather as an empirical sub-discipline: the sociology of mass communication, of education, of schools and of universities. Weber's sociology was a sociology of knowledge in the general sense of an approach to human interaction, to cultural institutions, to values, norms, motives and meanings, and in particular to their changes in history.

Finally, one could call Weber's sociology an 'historical sociology', or perhaps better a 'cultural sociology' (*Kultursoziologie*). (As to the latter see the brief excursus in the section 'Meaning and function', chapter 1.) What then are the main features of this 'cultural sociology'?

1 From De Tocqueville and Durkheim, to Weber, Simmel and Mannheim cultural sociologists have always been fascinated by the process of modernization. With a rather conservative concern, these sociologists were primarily interested in the often dramatic changes in values, norms, motives and meanings under the impact of industrialization, urbanization, the rise of science, technology and Capitalism (and its adversary: Marxism), and the rise of bureaucracy. They were interested in the impact of these changes on human groups and individuals, and they were normatively concerned about the future of humanity in a fully modernized society. Whereas 'modern' sociologists seem to live and work pre-reflectively within the context of modernity, these cultural sociologists asked questions about it and subjected it to their often very detailed scrutiny. (It should be noted that societies which are modernizing on a grand scale, like Western Europe after the Second World War, or the nations of the Third World today, have generally no use for such concerns and their ensuing interpretations and theories. They stand in need of a useful, applicable social science. It is this very need and not its scientific superiority or significance which gave the main impetus to the predominance of 'modern' American sociology! However, when in a fully modernized society, like the USA in the 1950s and Western Europe in the 1960s, people begin to ask questions as to the quality of life, 'cultural sociology' begins to regain its lost relevance!)

2 Epistemologically, 'cultural sociology', as it has been developed in Germany, remained rooted in some basic tenets of neo-Kantianism, notably in a profound scepsis with regard to Anglo-Saxon empiricism and its assumption of a possible correspondence between theory and reality. Weber's concepts are constructed ideal types which do not correspond at all to reality, but which will yet hopefully yield a rational understanding after they have been confronted with the experience of reality.

3 Methodologically, 'cultural sociology' does not shun speculation. Ideal types can be constructed in principle, although not always in actual fact, without empirical research. The speculative method of the thought-experiment is consciously applied.

4 The verification or falsification of its theories is not brought about by a confrontation of the ideal types with 'facts'. Ideal types have a heuristic nature. That is, the question is not whether they are 'true', but whether they are 'relevant' – i.e. whether they bring about a rational understanding (*Verstehen*) of socio-cultural reality.

5 The cultural sociologist will constantly hold discussions with others, but when he is at work, when he formulates his interpretations and theories, he will be alone. The construction of his concepts and theories does not primarily depend on technical skill (cf. the application of standard techniques in 'modern' sociology), but on his socio-cultural sensitivity, on his artistic skill to formulate ideas. As a result, his research is not reproducible.

6 Finally, the rationality to which the cultural sociologist aspires is generally of a substantial and not of a functional nature (for this distinction see chapter 1, p. 24). He does not aspire to be useful to policy in a functional manner, but rather tries to enlarge the rational understanding of socio-cultural reality. That is, he will try to enlighten himself and his fellow citizens by means of his observations and interpretations. His usefulness is of a heuristic rather than of a pragmatic nature.

An important additional feature of 'cultural sociology', at least in its Weberian variety, is its emphasis on the need of so-called 'value-freedom'. This is not 'ethical neutrality' or 'objectivity' as these have been conceived in 'modern' sociology. This Weberian 'value-freedom' should, to begin with, be tied closely to 'value-relevance' (*Wertbeziehung*). Second, it should be viewed as the conscious refusal to evaluate normatively the values in which the people one is studying happen to believe (*Wertungsfreiheit*). That is, the sociologist is related to values and meanings and it is the relevance of these values and meanings which help him to differentiate in socio-cultural reality between relevant and irrelevant facts. But when he sets out to study and interpret these relevant facts, he should impose upon himself the discipline not to evaluate them in terms of the values he himself happens to believe in: he should then consciously bracket his own convictions and beliefs.

It is at this point that my notion of a 'cultural analysis' beyond 'cultural sociology' enters into the discussion. It is my contention that we should engage in a systematic analysis of the above-mentioned value-relevance not just for ethical but also for scientific reasons. Weber has called this *Wertanalyse* (value analysis) but he always refused to engage in such an analysis (cf. the end of his essay on Protestant ethics and the spirit of Capitalism). He probably shunned it because he was afraid to end up in a normative philosophy, which in his time was the main field of operation for rather confused Hegelians. This, it seems to me, is an understandable but insufficient reason for abstaining from the task of cultural analysis.

In cultural analysis we explicitly discuss those values, norms, motives and meanings in our cultural orbit which we deem to be important, significant, typical, culturally 'healthy' or culturally 'pathological'. In other words, beyond cultural sociology (i.e. after we have engaged in cultural sociology thoroughly), we set out to analyse and interpret culture normatively. However, this does not necessarily mean that we engage in a rather old-fashioned kind of metaphysical social philosophy which usually leads to some form of cultural pessimism. In my *The Abstract Society* (1970), to give an example, I constructed a normative anthropological model (man as *homo duplex*), based on some tenets in the writings of Mead, Durkheim, Gehlen and others. I then analysed modern society ('abstract society') mainly in terms of Weber's routinization and rationalization thesis, and tried to demonstrate that man as a *homo duplex* is endangered by the process of modernization: he is gradually torn apart into a *homo internus* (modern subjectivism) and a *homo externus* (functional role player). While writing it and the present analysis of the cliché, which is itself another example of cultural analysis, I was fully aware of the fact that such an approach is not really appreciated nowadays, due to the predominance of the natural-scientific model of 'modern' sociology. But the one thing that the cultural sociologist should learn very early is not to care for the fads and fashions of modern civilization.

I fully realize that these brief remarks may give rise to more questions than can possibly be answered here; it would require another publication. I intended merely to provide the bare outlines of the theoretical frame of reference of the present study of clichés. We must now make a few additional comments about the crucial concepts used in this study.

Explication of some of the main concepts

The concept of modernity is a crucial cultural-sociological ideal type. It refers to the socio-psychological and cultural dimensions of modernization. Modernity is the mentality of modern man. It is the set of values, norms, motives and meanings, constituting a moral ethos which conditions individual behaviour (Weber's *Geist*, Durkheim's *conscience collective*). Modernity becomes sociologically 'visible' in modern society's institutions and the institutionalized behaviour of modern individuals. One could, of course, empirically analyse modernity by constructing scales (of anomie, alienation and boredom) and by testing representative samples of individuals in various modernized societies. One could, thus, admittedly arrive at some scientifically significant 'if-then propositions'. The question, however, is whether one indeed acquires in this way a substantially rational understanding of modernity as a specific historical pheno-menon. One has dissected a dead frog and the remainders of such a vivisection are unrelated bits and pieces which do not at all facilitate the emergence of rational *Verstehen*. As scientifically important as such operations may be, the question of what modernity is as an historically specific mentality and ethos cannot be answered in this way. Cultural sociology, and beyond it cultural analysis, may come much closer to an answer. They require, however, other methods and another theoretical frame of reference.

Durkheim once defined institutions, which he also called 'social facts', as traditional patterns of behaviour, as patterns of emotion, volition, action and speech which are handed over from generation to generation relatively independently of individuals. They thus may be looked upon sociologically as if they were autonomous realities ('facts'), constituting an autonomous, collective conscious-ness and conscience. Hence, if one wishes to study sociologically the mentality and ethos of an historically given society, one should focus on its institutions. In the present study, the concept of institu-tion is employed in this sense, and it is argued that the cliché is a very similar phenomenon. Exclusively for expediency's sake, the concepts of cognition, emotion, volition and action have been taken together into the concept of behaviour which, therefore, has a semantic content that differs from the standard, American meaning of the word behaviour. The concept of action refers to individual acts and social interactions both, while the concept of behaviour also includes cognition, emotion and volition. Language, or perhaps better, speech, has been kept separate from behaviour in order to emphasize the fact that clichés are not linguistic by nature, as is generally believed.

Every scientific discipline necessarily develops and employs its own jargon and clichés – a fact usually covered up by means of the imposing concept of 'paradigm'. It is argued in this book that clichés are indispensable in daily and scientific discourse. Yet, we should consciously try to limit their use. This, it seems to me, is not done by sociologists; one only has to randomly leaf through any issue of a sociological journal. Eric Partridge, that venerable British specialist of curious linguistic phenomena, complained recently about the 'pitiable socio-psychological jargon of American professors' (*Time*, 17 October, 1977, p. 57). He could, of course, have included socio-scientific professors of other nations as well, such as the French neo-Marxist and non-Marxist structuralists, or the adepts of the German Frankfurt School. As to the present study, I have not been able to avoid 'sociologese' (Fowler), but I have made an honest attempt to restrict its usage as much as possible. If sociologese happens to have been unavoidable, I have tried to explain as clearly as possible the meaning of its concepts.

Finally, I use this opportunity to comment briefly on the guiding notion of modern society as an 'abstract society'. In my book of that title I tried to give a cultural analysis of the abstract nature of contemporary society, re-formulating the sociological ideas inherent in such concepts as anomie and alienation. If I were now to re-write it, I would pay more attention to the political dimensions of abstract society, and would also include a discussion of Karl Popper's theory of abstract society (cf. *The Open Society and Its Enemies*, vol. 2, London, Routledge & Kegan Paul, 1952, pp. 174–76), which coincides remarkably with my own. When I wrote the book at the end of the 1960s, I was still very much a 'cultured despiser' (Schleiermacher) of everything political. By now I have been cured of this contempt for politics, albeit only partially and with reluctance. As to Popper's brief statement on the abstract society, regretfully I read it only one week after my own work had gone to the printer. As Popper correctly indicates, the notion of abstract society has far reaching consequences for the sociological discipline which still focuses too much on concrete groups, structures, organizations and institutions. The consequences are, I think, particularly drastic for the sociology of knowledge – which Popper, incidentally, has identified too much with the writings of Karl Mannheim. In any case, ever since Marx and Mannheim, the sociology of knowledge has knit 'knowledge' tightly to socio-economic and socio-cultural 'reality'. In modern abstract society, however, values, norms, motives and meanings – and not as Mannheim believed, the intelligentsia (following Alfred Weber) – have become free-floating and gratuitous. In such a situation 'knowledge' can no longer be linked directly and tightly to 'reality'. We cannot, of course, discuss here the implications of this fact for the sociology of knowledge, but its impact on the main argument of the present study has been great.

Notes

Introduction

1 Cf. Randall Collins and Michael Makowsky, *The Discovery of Society*, New York, Random House, 1972.

2 Quoted from Martin Gardner, 'The Holes in Black Holes', *New York Review of Books*, vol. 24, no. 15, 29 September 1977, p. 22. Gardner argues correctly that much of the public interest in these astrophysical topics is caused by contemporary metaphysical yearnings, rather than by a genuine interest in science.

3 Cf. Collins and Makowsky, op. cit., p. 4.

4 Max Scheler's concept of *Geist* comes very close to such a view of culture. To him *Geist* is the totality of 'ideal factors' as embodied by science, art, literature, music and law. From this metaphysically conceived totality only a certain portion will be realized in an historically specific society. The 'real factors' as embodied by the instincts and the institutional sectors based on them (state, marriage–family, economy) determine which components of the *Geist* will become reality in a given period of history. These 'real factors' thus function as a kind of sieve, formally analogous to the *a priori* categories of Kant's epistemology. Cf. Max Scheler, *Die Wissensformen und die Gesellschaft*, Bern, Francke Verlag, 1960, pp. 15–190.

5 Mannheim sensed this, when he wrote: 'It is possible, therefore, that in the future, in a world in which there is never anything new, in which all is finished and each moment is a repetition of the past, there can exist a condition in which thought will be utterly devoid of all ideological and utopian elements.' Karl Mannheim, *Ideology and Utopia*, (1936) trans. by L. Wirth and E. Shils, New York, Harcourt, Brace & World, n.d., p. 262.

6 Arnold Gehlen, 'Über kulturelle Kristallisation', in *Studien zur Anthropologie und Soziologie*, Neuwied-Berlin, Luchterhand Verlag, 1963, pp. 311–28. See for his notion of 'post-histoire' his essay 'Ende der Geschichte?', in *Einblicke*, Frankfurt am Main, Klostermann Verlag, 1975, pp. 115–34.

114

7 In his well-known lecture *De nostri temporis studiorum ratione* (1709) G. Vico said:

> Our modern physicists remind me of certain individuals who have inherited from their parents a gorgeous mansion leaving nothing to be desired in point of comfort and luxury. There is nothing left for them to do except to move the furniture around, and by slight modifications, add some ornaments and bring things up to date (*On the Study Methods of our Time*, trans. by E. Gianturco, New York, Bobbs-Merrill, 1965, p. 21).

8 This stands in contrast with Max Weber's notion of the unavoidably eternal youth of the historical (socio-cultural) sciences, due to the fact that life, history, culture flow onwards eternally:

> The stream of immeasurable events flows unendingly towards eternity. The cultural problems which move men form themselves ever anew and in different colours, and the boundaries of that area in the infinite stream of concrete events which acquires meaning and significance for us, i.e. which becomes an 'historical individual', are constantly subject to change. The intellectual contexts from which it is viewed and scientifically analysed shift. The points of departure of the cultural sciences remain changeable throughout the limitless future as long as a Chinese ossification of intellectual life does not render mankind incapable of setting new questions to the eternally inexhaustible flow of life.

The quotation is from Weber's ' "Objectivity" in Social Science and Social Policy', *The Methodology of the Social Sciences*, trans. by E. A. Shils and H. A. Finch, Chicago, Free Press, 1949, p. 84. On p. 104 the notion of the 'eternal youth' of the socio-cultural sciences is mentioned. Weber does not indicate here under which conditions such 'Chinese ossification of intellectual life' could at all come about. We know, however, that he was very much afraid that modern bureaucracy would eventually lead to such an intellectually stifling situation. Incidentally, in these rather romantic passages Weber follows some irrational tenets of the so-called 'philosophy of life' (*Lebensphilosophie*) which got a hold on neo-Kantianism in the wake of the notion of 'das Ding-an-sich'. They contrast, in my opinion, strongly with the generally rational tenet of Weber's sociology.

9 H. W. Fowler, *A Dictionary of Modern English Usage*, revised edition by Sir E. Gowers, Oxford, Clarendon Press, 1977, p. 91.

Chapter 1 Clichés defined

1 *The Compact Edition of The Oxford English Dictionary*, New York, Oxford University Press, 1973, p. 434, s.v. cliché.
2 Ibid., p. 3924, s.v. cliché.
3 *The Random House Dictionary of the English Language*, New York, Random House, 1967, p. 276, s.v. cliché. As will become clear later, I strongly disagree with the idea that clichés have lost impact.

4 Ibid., p. 297.
5 *Oxford English Dictionary* p. 1237.
6 H. W. Fowler, *A Dictionary of Modern English Usage*, revised edition by Sir E. Gowers, Oxford, Clarendon Press, 1977, p. 234, s.v. hackneyed phrases.
7 G. I. Nierenberg and H. H. Calero, *Meta-Talk*, New York, Simon & Schuster, 1973.
8 Muzafer Sherif, 'The Psychology of Slogans', in *Social Interaction*, Chicago, Aldine Publishing Co., 1967, p. 154.
9 H. W. Fowler, op. cit., p. 235, s.v. hackneyed phrases. Cf. Eric Partridge, *A Dictionary of Catch Phrases, British and American, from the Sixteenth Century to the present day*, London, Routledge & Kegan Paul, 1977. Anthony Burgess wrote a delightful review of this book: 'Twixt proverb and quote', *Times Literary Supplement*, 26 August 1977, p. 1027. Burgess ends by saying: 'Homage to Eric Partridge in his word-tree, and may he live for ever and me live to bury him.' Cf. also Philip Howard, *New Words for Old: A Survey of Misused, Vogue and Cliché Words*, London, Hamish Hamilton, 1977.
10 Arnold Gehlen has discussed this transference of meaning, within the context of his theory of institutions, in terms of a fundamental distinction between '*Motiv und Zweck*' in human behaviour. Cf. his *Urmensch und Spätkultur*, Bonn, Athenaeum Verlag, 1956. In an oral communication, Anton Bevers (Nijmegen) pointed out to me that the supersedure of meaning by function in modernization plays a very crucial role. See also Georg Simmel's *Philosophie des Geldes*, Berlin, Duncker & Humblot, 1958, sixth edition (English edition: G. Simmel, *Philosophy of Money*, London, Routledge & Kegan Paul, 1978).
11 Rickert formulated his epistemological and methodological ideas in his study *Die Grenzen der naturwissenschaftlichen Begriffsbildung*, (1896), Tübingen, Mohr–Siebeck, 1929, fifth edition. An abbreviated version can be found in his *Kulturwissenschaft und Naturwissenschaft* (1898), Tübingen, Mohr–Siebeck, 1915, third edition.
12 Cf. Karl Mannheim, *Man and Society in an Age of Reconstruction* (1940), London, Routledge & Kegan Paul, 1960, p. 53.
13 Cf. Peter L. Berger, *The Sacred Canopy*, New York, Doubleday, 1967. This elaborates the Weberian notion of theodicy.

Chapter 2   The clichégenic society

1 *Montreal Star*, 28 September 1977, p. F-7.
2 *The Random House Dictionary of the 'English Language*, New York, Random House, 1967, s.v. slang, p. 1338. This gives the |follow-ing description of slang:

> 1. very informal usage in vocabulary and idiom that is characteristically more metaphorical, playful, elliptical, vivid, and ephemeral, than ordinary language, as 'Hit the road'. 2. (in English and some other languages) speech and writing characterized by the use of vulgar and socially taboo vocabulary and idiomatic expressions. 3. the jargon of a

particular class, profession, etc. 4. the special vocabulary of thieves, vagabonds, etc.; argot.

In (3) and (4) clichés will naturally play a central role. It is quite possible that slang, as defined under (1), constitutes a rich source for our more informal and 'vulgar' clichés. That is, we might find here the empirical origin of a certain type of cliché. In the present study, however, the problem of the historical and empirical origins of clichés (as well as their categorization) will, for various reasons, not be dealt with.

3 *Montreal Star*, op. cit.
4 Walter Benjamin, *Illuminations*, Hannah Arendt (ed.), New York, Schocken Books, 1969, p. 223.
5 Ibid.
6 It is significant, in the present context, that an object of art which possesses aura demands a very specific physical environment. One cannot, for example, just hang it on any wall, or place it in any room, next to other works of art, and it demands very specific shades of light.
7 Benjamin, op. cit.
8 Cf. for Benjamin's own discussion of Brecht's 'epic theatre' 'What is Epic Theatre?' in *Illuminations*, pp. 147–54. Also Benjamin's *Understanding Brecht*, trans. Anna Bostock (1966), London, New Left Books, 1973. This volume contains two versions of the essay 'What is Epic Theatre?'
9 Cf. Wolfgang Mommsen, *The Age of Bureaucracy*, Oxford, Blackwell, 1974.
10 In a modernized society like the USA, franchising has greatly contributed to the uniformity of American food. The hamburger, everywhere the same on the North-American continent, is the universal symbol of this fact. Cf. George F. Will, 'Art of the Hamburger', *Newsweek*, 20 February 1978, p. 96. The author makes the following amusing observation: 'Europeans linger over meals; Americans regard food as fuel to be taken in the way steam locomotives took on water, scooping it at full speed from troughs between the rails. This vast and polyglot nation has never pretended to have a national cuisine. Americans generally want food that is hygienic, copious and fast.'
11 Cf. 'Denim in the '70s: From Rags to Riches', *Gazette*, 22 March 1978, section 'Consumer Spotlight', p. 1. I shall argue later that clichés may provide the modern individual with some degree of certainty and stability in a basically vague and abstract society. In this respect the following observation, made in this small article, is quite relevant: 'Jeans have come to represent ... security in an insecure fashion world, a solid base to wear as you will, a lump of clay to hold as you will, a uniform or an expression.' The article ends with this statement: 'Some people use jeans to make a statement about status, while others wear jeans to melt into the crowd. In short, a magic costume. Now one thing, now another.'
12 *New York Times*, 21 August 1977, p. D-14. Karl Popper distinguishes in his intellectual autobiography similarly between 'subjective' and

'objective' music, but he applies this to compositions rather than performances. Cf. his 'Two kinds of music', in *Unended Quest* (1974) Glasgow, Collins-Fontana, 1976, pp. 60–7.

13 I have discussed this point in greater detail in my study on humour and laughter: *Humor und Gesellschaft*, Graz, Vienna, Cologne, Styria Verlag, 1976, pp. 143–72.

14 For an elaborate discussion of these and related issues see 'Autonomy in a Pluralistic Society', chapter 5 of my *The Abstract Society*, New York, Doubleday, 1970; Harmondsworth, Penguin, 1973, pp. 127–42.

15 W. I. Thomas, *The Unadjusted Girl* (1928), New York, Harper Torch-books, 1967, p. 82.

16 In chapter 4 of *The Abstract Society* I distinguished three ideal types of protest: Gnosticism, anarchism and activism. See pp. 85–126.

17 *Ladies' Home Journal*, vol. 96, no. 9, September 1977, pp. 34–44.

18 Ibid., p. 40.

19 Hilton Kramer, 'The Triumph of Misreading', *New York Times Review of Books*, 21 August 1977, p. 3.

20 Arnold Gehlen, *Urmensch und Spätkultur*, Bonn, Athenaeum Verlag, 1956.

21 Helmuth Schelsky, '*Ist die Dauerreflexion institutionalisierbar?*' 1957, in *Auf der Suche nach Wirklichkeit*, Düsseldorf, Cologne, Diederichs Verlag, 1965, pp 250–75.

22 I added 'temporarily' in order to stress the fact that clichés are not tied to any long-term, traditional commitment. They are easily picked up and as easily discarded.

23 Cf. Theodor Adorno, *The Jargon of Authenticity* (1964) trans. by K. Tarnowski and F. Will, London, Routledge & Kegan Paul, 1973. On p. 10 Adorno writes: 'Those who have run out of holy spirit speak with mechanical tongues.'

24 The 'classic' philosopher of immorality is, of course, Friedrich Nietzsche. His notion of 'beyond good and evil' is a symptomatic example of ethics in abstract society. The Austrian novelist Robert Musil described it impressively in his *Der Mann Ohne Eigenschaften* ('*The Man Without Qualities*').

25 Cf. in this context Milan Machovec, *A Marxist Looks at Jesus*, London, Darton, Longmann & Todd, 1976.

26 Donald E. Smith (ed.), *Religion, Politics, and Social Change in the Third World: A Sourcebook*, New York, Free Press, 1971, p. 250.

27 For a detailed discussion of this point see again my *The Abstract Society*, chapter 5.

Chapter 3   Clichés unbound

1 Cf. Ervin Goffman, *Frame Analysis*, New York, Harper & Row, 1974.

2 Cf. Otto Mann, *Der Dandy* (1925), Heidelberg, W. Rothe Verlag, 1962. Cf. also Hubert Cole, *Beau Brummell*, St Albans, Hart-Davis, Mc-Gibbon, 1976.

3 See for many examples: David Sudnow, *Passing On: The Social Organization of Dying*, Englewood Cliffs, NJ, Prentice-Hall, 1967, in particular chapter 5, 'On Bad News', pp. 117–52.

4 Helmuth Plessner, *Lachen und Weinen* (1941) in *Philosophische Anthropologie*, Frankfurt am Main, Fischer Verlag, 1970, pp. 11–171.
5 Arnold Gehlen, *Urmensch und Spätkultur*, Bonn, Athenaeum Verlag, 1956. Cf. also his essay 'Über die Verstehbarkeit der Magie', in *Studien zur Anthropologie und Soziologie*, Neuwied-Berlin, Luchterhand Verlag, 1963, pp. 79–92.
6 George Orwell, *The Collected Essays, Journalism and Letters*, vol. 4, Harmondsworth, Penguin, 1971, p. 162. Elsewhere in this essay Orwell compares clichés to 'a packet of aspirins always at one's elbow' (p. 167). Discussing the clichés of a political pamphlet he had just received with the morning's post, he writes: '[these] words, like the cavalry horses answering the bugle, group themselves automatically into the familiar dreary pattern.' (Ibid.)
7 A. N. J. den Hollander, 'Ongerief van de Verwoording', in *Visie en Verantwoording*, Assen, Van Gorcum, 1968, p. 73.
8 H. W. Fowler, *A Dictionary of Modern English Usage*, revised edition by Sir E. Gowers, Oxford, Clarendon Press, 1977, p. 91, s.v. cliché.
9 I have discussed this mechanism with regard to jokes in my *Humor und Gesellschaft*, Graz, Vienna, Cologne, Styria Verlag, 1976. I do not find it necessary to discuss the obvious link between clichés and labelling. The classic statement in the so-called 'labelling theory' is H. S. Becker's *Outsiders: Studies in the Sociology of Deviance* (1963) New York, The Free Press, 1966. This book and most of the literature on deviance that followed, demonstrates clearly the importance of the cliché and its functionality in the mechanism of labelling.
10 H. W. Fowler, op. cit., pp. 306 ff., s.v. irrelevant allusions.
11 Ibid., p. 306.
12 Cf. *The Random House Dictionary of the English Language*, New York, Random House, 1967, p. 764, s.v. jargon.
13 H. W. Fowler, op. cit., p. 570, s.v. sociologese.

Chapter 4 Clichés and boredom

1 Parts of this chapter have been published previously in my 'Modernisierung und Langweile', in Oskar Schatz (ed.), *Was wird aus dem Menschen?*, Graz, Vienna, Cologne, Styria Verlag, 1975, pp. 321–37.
2 Cf. Stuart Hampshire, 'The Future of Knowledge', *New York Review of Books*, vol. 24, no. 5, 31 March 1977, p. 18:

> The essence of work, or of mere work, is, and always has been, repetition. But over most of known history the repetitions have been given significance by recurring celebrations of seasons and of work done, in feasts, ceremonies, enactments of myth and history, dramatic and musical performances, public manifestations of all kinds.

> Without such celebrations, the repetitions of work leave 'a blank, an empty aging, an undifferentiated stretch of days and months, as in a prison before death'. In such a situation, Hampshire concludes correctly, boredom will reign.

3 Baudelaire spoke of boredom with fear, almost as a man begging not to be seized by it, for he felt that it drove him through the despair of meaninglessness to complete irresponsibility. A bored man, he said, would willingly reduce the world to debris (César Grana, *Modernity and Its Discontents* (1964), New York, Harper & Row, 1967, p. 129).

In this context, Oscar Wilde's insightful picture of Thomas G. Waineright (1794–1852), dandy and murderer, gains special relevance. Cf. his 'Pen, Pencil and Poison', in *Complete Works of Oscar Wilde* (1948) London, Collins, 1969, pp. 993–1008.

4. For this passage on Hegel's theory of boredom I have relied on Eric Voegelin, 'On Hegel – A Study in Sorcery', *Studium Generale*, no. 24, 1971, pp. 335–58.

5 The literature on Gnosticism is by now very extensive. The following bibliographical items are, in my opinion, of interest to the sociologist: Hans Jonas, *The Gnostic Religion*, Boston, Beacon Press, 1963, which has recently been reprinted; Gilles Quispel, *Gnosis als Weltreligion*, Zürich, Origo Verlag, 1952; Eric Voegelin, *Science, Politics and Gnosticism*, Chicago, Henry Regnery Co., 1968; Eric Voegelin, *The New Science of Politics* (1952) University of Chicago Press, 1969; Ernst Topitsch, 'Marxismus und Gnosis', in *Sozialphilosophie zwischen Ideologie und Wissenschaft*, Neuwied-Berlin, Luchterhand Verlag, 1961, pp. 235–71. Cf. also my *The Abstract Society*, pp. 96–102.

6 In another publication I have called this modern man's 'anti-institutional mood'; cf. 'The Anti-Institutional Mood', *Worldview*, vol. 15, no. 9, September 1972, pp. 32–6.

7 Anton Chekhov, *Three Sisters*, in *Four Great Plays by Chekhov*, trans. by Constance Garnett, New York, Bantam Books, 1968, sixteenth edition, pp. 124 ff. Seen against the background of Chekhov's total *oeuvre*, it is quite obvious that this remark, often quoted by Soviet ideologues, has little to do with an early-Marxist or pre-Marxist critique of decadent, bourgeois, tsarist society. The yearning for hard work and for a revolutionary change in society is rather inspired by boredom and by a romantic–aesthetic longing for deliverance. This was very well analysed by César Grana (op. cit.). We cannot discuss here the intrinsic relationship between boredom and wit. Obviously, humour and wit are tedium-breaking devices consciously used by various authors, sometimes in a subtle manner (Chekhov), sometimes rather blatantly (Wilde, Waugh). Cf. Alvin Redman (ed.), *The Wit and Humor of Oscar Wilde* (1952) New York, Dover Publications, 1959. For a description of Evelyn Waugh's boredom cf. Frances Donaldson, *Evelyn Waugh*, New York, Chilton Book Co., 1967, pp. 22 ff., 30 and 78. As to clichés, Waugh once formulated the following advice: 'One cannot avoid clichés . . . , but one should not lead up to them' (bid., p. 34).

8 Cf. Peter Goldman and Gerald Lubenov, 'Where the Flowers Have Gone', *Newsweek*, 5 September 1977, pp. 24–30.

9 *Montreal Star*, 12 September 1977, p. C-13. This review is obviously written in 'disc-jockey language' which generally applies what may be

called the verbal bombardment: its words try to be as loud, hyperbolic and emotionally stimulating as the music it wants to describe. Needless to say, such language is highly clichégenic.

10 This is, of course, also very much the case in Marxist countries. Cf. David K. Shipler, 'In Russia, the Revolutionary Dream Has Run its Course', *New York Times*, 6 November 1977, p. E-5. The author argues that the Marxist ideology functions in present day Russia as a set of reflexes, but it does no longer

> shape the direction of change inside society. It has atrophied into a set of slogans and symbols often used to camouflage anti-Marxist practices and to elicit stereotyped interpretations of events at home and abroad. 'There is just barrenness, complete ideological stagnation,' said a Soviet scholar. 'You can read any book [now published on ideology] in 20 minutes. To be a creative ideologist now means to be in opposition. It is easier to be a creative Communist in Spain or Italy than in the USSR.'

The situation in China, we may assume, is not much different (cf. the *Little Red Book* with Maoist slogans and clichés launched for manipulatory reasons). (See the introduction to chapter 5 of this volume.)

11 This dimension should be added to Kateb's insightful discussion of contemporary nihilism. Cf. George Kateb, 'The Next Stage of Nihilism', *Social Research*, vol. 40, no. 3, Autumn 1973, pp. 468–80.

12 The fascist nature of this ultra-left terrorism was also emphasized by Jillian Becker, *Hitler's Children: The Story of the Baader-Meinhof Gang*, London, Michael Joseph, 1977. Regretfully I was unable to read this before the present study went into print. My attention was drawn to it by Robert S. Wistrich's review: 'From Satire to the Machine-Gun', *Times Literary Supplement*, 26 August 1977, p. 1031. Wistrich's ends by saying: 'They [i.e. the ultra-left, German terrorists] would have done well to ponder on Albert Camus's maxim in *The Rebel*: "Every form of contempt, if it intervenes in politics, prepares the way for, or establishes, Fascism." ' Cf. also Barbara Beck, 'Dr. Marcuse's Children?' *Encounter*, vol. 50, no. 2, February 1978, pp. 74–77.

Chapter 5   Clichés bound

1 Peter L. Berger, *The Precarious Vision*, New York, Doubleday, 1961.

2 Cf. R. K. Merton, 'Puritanism, Pietism and Science' in *Social Theory and Social Structure* (1949), New York and London, Macmillan, 1957, revised and enlarged edition, pp. 574–606.

3 G. H. Mead, *Movements of Thought in the Nineteenth Century* (1936), University of Chicago Press, 1962, p. 5.

4 Thomas S. Kuhn, *The Structure of Scientific Revolutions* (1962) second and enlarged edition, University of Chicago Press, 1973. It is quite illuminating to re-read this much discussed book in the light of the present analysis of clichés. On science and puzzle-solving, cf. pp. 35–42.

5 For a good discussion of the Copernican world-views, see Jerzy Neyman (ed.), *The Heritage of Copernicus*, Cambridge, Mass., MIT Press, 1974.

6 A very good description of this is given by Ernest Jones in his biography of Freud (particularly in the first two volumes). Cf. Ernest Jones, *The Life and Work of Sigmund Freud*, vol. 1, 1953; vol. 2, 1955; vol. 3, 1957, New York, Basic Books, 1953–7.

7 Unintentionally Ernest Jones provides a very good picture of this process. See also Paul Roazen, *Brother Animal* (1969), Harmondsworth, Penguin, 1973.

8 A perfect example is offered by Taylor Branch, 'New Frontiers in American Philosophy', *New York Times Magazine*, 14 August 1977, pp. 12 ff. This article deals with a young American philosopher, 'described by a colleague as the "one true genius of our profession": "A prodigy of mathematics and logic, he is now beginning to address some of the most fundamental aspects of human experience" [sic!].' The author of this article, who uses many hyperbolic clichés, obviously tries to sell this 'analytic philosopher' ('yet so little known outside his his field', p. 13) to his readers as if he were a top producer. The article ends as follows:

> And then he smiles. He jokes that his greatest fear is that a philosopher at a convention many years hence will remark about some fellow named K. who was 'only a figure in the middle period of American philsophy'. He would rather be the founder of a new philosophy. By struggling with the nature of reality itself, philosophers have touched the most sublime and most absurd chords of the human ego. 'K. may want to build a whole cathedral', said a dazzled philosopher after the truth lecture [sic!], 'but I'd settle for one of his little stained-glass windows' (ibid., p. 67).

9 For the notion of 'intellectual asceticism' see my *The Abstract Society*, pp. 156–77.

10 The following discussion of kitsch and its clichés has benefited from an unpublished paper on so-called 'consumption literature' written by Vladimir Bina under my supervision. See also Gert Richter, *Kitsch-Lexikon Von A Bis Z*, Gutersloh-Berlin, Bertelsmann Verlag, 1972. The preface gives an excellent survey of the main characteristics of kitsch. Richter mentions the 'Klischeehaftigkeit' of kitsch, ibid., p. 11. A nicely illustrated and perceptive analysis of American kitsch is provided by Curtis F. Brown, *Star-Spangled Kitsch*, New York, Universe Books, 1975. Both books contain brief but helpful bibliographies.

11 Mahler never composed an opera, but he was a very skilled and famous opera conductor. In terms of the aesthetic sublimation of clichés, *opera* presents a particular interesting case. In most operas both the libretto and the plot are heavily loaded with clichés, while in many cases the music transcends them. The best examples are provided by Mozart's operas. As to Mahler, Jones writes in his

biography of Freud that he met Freud in Leyden during the summer of 1910. He then interpreted his music in a psycho-analytic manner:

In the course of the talk Mahler suddenly said that now he understood why his music had always been prevented from achieving the highest rank through the noblest passages, those inspired by the most profound emotions, being spoiled by the intrusion of some common-place melody. His father, apparently a brutal person, treated his wife very badly, and when Mahler was a young boy there was a specially painful scene between them. It became quite unbearable to the boy, who rushed away from the house. At that moment, however, a hurdy-gurdy in the street was grinding out the popular Viennese air 'Ach du lieber Augustin'. In Mahler's opinion the conjunction of high tragedy and light amusement was from then on inextricably fixed in his mind, and the one mood inevitably brought the other with it (Ernest Jones, op. cit., vol. 2, pp. 79 ff.).

It seems to me that Mahler got carried away by his enthusiasm for Freud and his psycho-analysis (like so many before and after him), when he came up with this interpretation of the banality component in his music.

12 Cf. my *Humor und Gesellschaft*, Graz, Vienna, Cologne, Styria Verlag, 1976; in particular pp. 21–50.
13 *Zote* means in German a *risqué* remark or joke of an erotic nature; Freud uses the word in this sense regularly. It comes close to (but is not exactly the same as) the Anglo-Saxon 'dirty joke'. As to the latter, cf. G. Legman, *Rationale of the Dirty Joke*, London, Jonathan Cape, n.d.
14 This had been the *Leitmotif* in my interpretation of the pre-modern ceremonial clown or buffoon. Cf. ibid., pp. 143–72.

Index

Routledge Social Science Series

Routledge & Kegan Paul   London, Henley and Boston

39 Store Street, London WC1E 7DD
Broadway House, Newtown Road, Henley-on-Thames,
Oxon RG9 1EN
9 Park Street, Boston, Mass. 02108

Contents

*Authors wishing to submit manuscripts for any series in
this catalogue should send them to the Social Science Editor,
Routledge & Kegan Paul Ltd, 39 Store Street,
London WC1E 7DD*

● *Books so marked are available in paperback*
All books are in Metric Demy 8vo format (216 × 138mm approx.)

International Library of Sociology

General Editor John Rex

GENERAL SOCIOLOGY

Barnsley, J. H. The Social Reality of Ethics. *464 pp.*
Belshaw, Cyril. The Conditions of Social Performance. *An Exploratory Theory. 144 pp.*
Brown, Robert. Explanation in Social Science. *208 pp.*
● Rules and Laws in Sociology. *192 pp.*
Bruford, W. H. Chekhov and His Russia. *A Sociological Study. 244 pp.*
Cain, Maureen E. Society and the Policeman's Role. *326 pp.*
●**Fletcher, Colin.** Beneath the Surface. *An Account of Three Styles of Sociological Research. 221 pp.*
Gibson, Quentin. The Logic of Social Enquiry. *240 pp.*
Glucksmann, M. Structuralist Analysis in Contemporary Social Thought. *212 pp.*
Gurvitch, Georges. Sociology of Law. *Preface by Roscoe Pound. 264 pp.*
Hodge, H. A. Wilhelm Dilthey. *An Introduction. 184 pp.*
Homans, George C. Sentiments and Activities. *336 pp.*
Johnson, Harry M. Sociology: *a Systematic Introduction. Foreword by Robert K. Merton. 710 pp.*
●**Keat, Russell,** and **Urry, John.** Social Theory as Science. *278 pp.*
Mannheim, Karl. Essays on Sociology and Social Psychology. *Edited by Paul Keckskemeti. With Editorial Note by Adolph Lowe. 344 pp.*
  Systematic Sociology: *An Introduction to the Study of Society. Edited by J. S. Erös and Professor W. A. C. Stewart. 220 pp.*
Martindale, Don, The Nature and Types of Sociological Theory. *292 pp.*
●**Maus, Heinz.** A Short History of Sociology. *234 pp.*
Mey, Harald. Field-Theory. *A Study of its Application in the Social Sciences. 352 pp.*
Myrdal, Gunnar. Value in Social Theory: *A Collection of Essays on Methodology. Edited by Paul Streeten. 332 pp.*
Ogburn, William F., and **Nimkoff, Meyer F.** A Handbook of Sociology. *Preface by Karl Mannheim. 656 pp. 46 figures. 35 tables.*
Parsons, Talcott, and **Smelser, Neil J.** Economy and Society: *A Study in the Integration of Economic and Social Theory. 362 pp.*
Podgórecki, Adam. Practical Social Sciences. *About 200 pp.*
●**Rex, John.** Key Problems of Sociological Theory. *220 pp.*
  Sociology and the Demystification of the Modern World. *282 pp.*
●**Rex, John** (Ed.) Approaches to Sociology. *Contributions by Peter Abell, Frank Bechhofer, Basil Bernstein, Ronald Fletcher, David Frisby, Miriam Glucksmann, Peter Lassman, Herminio Martins, John Rex, Roland Robertson, John Westergaard and Jock Young. 302 pp.*
Rigby, A. Alternative Realities. *352 pp.*
Roche, M. Phenomenology, Language and the Social Sciences. *374 pp.*

Sahay, A. Sociological Analysis. *220 pp.*
Simirenko, Alex (Ed.) Soviet Sociology. *Historical Antecedents and Current Appraisals. Introduction by Alex Simirenko. 376 pp.*
Strasser, Hermann. The Normative Structure of Sociology. *Conservative and Emancipatory Themes in Social Thought. About 340 pp.*
Urry, John. Reference Groups and the Theory of Revolution. *244 pp.*
Weinberg, E. Development of Sociology in the Soviet Union. *173 pp.*

FOREIGN CLASSICS OF SOCIOLOGY

●Durkheim, Emile. Suicide. *A Study in Sociology. Edited and with an Introduction by George Simpson. 404 pp.*
●Gerth, H. H., and Mills, C. Wright. From Max Weber: *Essays in Sociology. 502 pp.*
●Tönnies, Ferdinand. Community and Association. (*Gemeinschaft und Gesellschaft.) Translated and Supplemented by Charles P. Loomis. Foreword by Pitirim A. Sorokin. 334 pp.*

SOCIAL STRUCTURE

Andreski, Stanislav. Military Organization and Society. *Foreword by Professor A. R. Radcliffe-Brown. 226 pp. 1 folder.*
Carlton, Eric. Ideology and Social Order. *Preface by Professor Philip Abrahams. About 320 pp.*
Coontz, Sydney H. Population Theories and the Economic Interpretation. *202 pp.*
Coser, Lewis. The Functions of Social Conflict. *204 pp.*
Dickie-Clark, H. F. Marginal Situation: *A Sociological Study of a Coloured Group. 240 pp. 11 tables.*
Glaser, Barney, and Strauss, Anselm L. Status Passage. *A Formal Theory. 208 pp.*
Glass, D. V. (Ed.) Social Mobility in Britain. *Contributions by J. Berent, T. Bottomore, R. C. Chambers, J. Floud, D. V. Glass, J. R. Hall, H. T. Himmelweit, R. K. Kelsall, F. M. Martin, C. A. Moser, R. Mukherjee, and W. Ziegel. 420 pp.*
Johnstone, Frederick A. Class, Race and Gold. *A Study of Class Relations and Racial Discrimination in South Africa. 312 pp.*
Jones, Garth N. Planned Organizational Change: *An Exploratory Study Using an Empirical Approach. 268 pp.*
Kelsall, R. K. Higher Civil Servants in Britain: *From 1870 to the Present Day. 268 pp. 31 tables.*
König, René. The Community. *232 pp. Illustrated.*
●Lawton, Denis. Social Class, Language and Education. *192 pp.*
McLeish, John. The Theory of Social Change: *Four Views Considered. 128 pp.*
Marsh, David C. The Changing Social Structure of England and Wales, *1871-1961. 288 pp.*
Menzies, Ken. Talcott Parsons and the Social Image of Man. *About 208 pp.*

●**Mouzelis, Nicos.** Organization and Bureaucracy. *An Analysis of Modern Theories. 240 pp.*
Mulkay, M. J. Functionalism, Exchange and Theoretical Strategy. *272 pp.*
Ossowski, Stanislaw. Class Structure in the Social Consciousness. *210 pp.*
●**Podgórecki, Adam.** Law and Society. *302 pp.*
Renner, Karl. Institutions of Private Law and Their Social Functions. *Edited, with an Introduction and Notes, by O. Kahn-Freud. Translated by Agnes Schwarzschild. 316 pp.*

SOCIOLOGY AND POLITICS

Acton, T. A. Gypsy Politics and Social Change. *316 pp.*
Clegg, Stuart. Power, Rule and Domination. *A Critical and Empirical Understanding of Power in Sociological Theory and Organisational Life. About 300 pp.*
Hechter, Michael. Internal Colonialism. *The Celtic Fringe in British National Development, 1536–1966. 361 pp.*
Hertz, Frederick. Nationality in History and Politics: *A Psychology and Sociology of National Sentiment and Nationalism. 432 pp.*
Kornhauser, William. The Politics of Mass Society. *272 pp. 20 tables.*
●**Kroes, R.** Soldiers and Students. *A Study of Right- and Left-wing Students. 174 pp.*
Laidler, Harry W. History of Socialism. *Social-Economic Movements: An Historical and Comparative Survey of Socialism, Communism, Co-operation, Utopianism; and other Systems of Reform and Reconstruction. 992 pp.*
Lasswell, H. D. Analysis of Political Behaviour. *324 pp.*
Martin, David A. Pacifism: *an Historical and Sociological Study. 262 pp.*
Martin, Roderick. Sociology of Power. *About 272 pp.*
Myrdal, Gunnar. The Political Element in the Development of Economic Theory. *Translated from the German by Paul Streeten. 282 pp.*
Wilson, H. T. The American Ideology. *Science, Technology and Organization of Modes of Rationality. About 280 pp.*
Wootton, Graham. Workers, Unions and the State. *188 pp.*

CRIMINOLOGY

Ancel, Marc. Social Defence: *A Modern Approach to Criminal Problems. Foreword by Leon Radzinowicz. 240 pp.*
Cain, Maureen E. Society and the Policeman's Role. *326 pp.*
Cloward, Richard A., and **Ohlin, Lloyd E.** Delinquency and Opportunity: *A Theory of Delinquent Gangs. 248 pp.*
Downes, David M. The Delinquent Solution. *A Study in Subcultural Theory. 296 pp.*
Dunlop, A. B., and **McCabe, S.** Young Men in Detention Centres. *192 pp.*
Friedlander, Kate. The Psycho-Analytical Approach to Juvenile Delinquency: *Theory, Case Studies, Treatment. 320 pp.*
Glueck, Sheldon, and **Eleanor.** Family Environment and Delinquency. *With the statistical assistance of Rose W. Kneznek. 340 pp.*

Lopez-Rey, Manuel. Crime. *An Analytical Appraisal. 288 pp.*

Mannheim, Hermann. Comparative Criminology: *a Text Book. Two volumes. 442 pp. and 380 pp.*

Morris, Terence. The Criminal Area: *A Study in Social Ecology. Foreword by Hermann Mannheim. 232 pp. 25 tables. 4 maps.*

Rock, Paul. Making People Pay. *338 pp.*

●**Taylor, Ian, Walton, Paul,** and **Young, Jock.** The New Criminology. *For a Social Theory of Deviance. 325 pp.*

●**Taylor, Ian, Walton, Paul,** and **Young, Jock** (Eds). Critical Criminology. *268 pp.*

SOCIAL PSYCHOLOGY

Bagley, Christopher. The Social Psychology of the Epileptic Child. *320 pp.*

Barbu, Zevedei. Problems of Historical Psychology. *248 pp.*

Blackburn, Julian. Psychology and the Social Pattern. *184 pp.*

●**Brittan, Arthur.** Meanings and Situations. *224 pp.*

Carroll, J. Break-Out from the Crystal Palace. *200 pp.*

●**Fleming, C. M.** Adolescence: Its Social Psychology. *With an Introduction to recent findings from the fields of Anthropology, Physiology, Medicine, Psychometrics and Sociometry. 288 pp.*

● The Social Psychology of Education: *An Introduction and Guide to Its Study. 136 pp.*

●**Homans, George C.** The Human Group. *Foreword by Bernard DeVoto. Introduction by Robert K. Merton. 526 pp.*

● Social Behaviour: *its Elementary Forms. 416 pp.*

●**Klein, Josephine.** The Study of Groups. *226 pp. 31 figures. 5 tables.*

Linton, Ralph. The Cultural Background of Personality. *132 pp.*

●**Mayo, Elton.** The Social Problems of an Industrial Civilization. *With an appendix on the Political Problem. 180 pp.*

Ottaway, A. K. C. Learning Through Group Experience. *176 pp.*

Plummer, Ken. Sexual Stigma. *An Interactionist Account. 254 pp.*

●**Rose, Arnold M.** (Ed.) Human Behaviour and Social Processes: *an Interactionist Approach. Contributions by Arnold M. Rose, Ralph H. Turner, Anselm Strauss, Everett C. Hughes, E. Franklin Frazier, Howard S. Becker, et al. 696 pp.*

Smelser, Neil J. Theory of Collective Behaviour. *448 pp.*

Stephenson, Geoffrey M. The Development of Conscience. *128 pp.*

Young, Kimball. Handbook of Social Psychology. *658 pp. 16 figures. 10 tables.*

SOCIOLOGY OF THE FAMILY

Banks, J. A. Prosperity and Parenthood: *A Study of Family Planning among The Victorian Middle Classes. 262 pp.*

Bell, Colin R. Middle Class Families: *Social and Geographical Mobility. 224 pp.*

Burton, Lindy. Vulnerable Children. *272 pp.*
Gavron, Hannah. The Captive Wife: *Conflicts of Household Mothers.* *190 pp.*
George, Victor, and **Wilding, Paul.** Motherless Families. *248 pp.*
Klein, Josephine. Samples from English Cultures.
  1. Three Preliminary Studies and Aspects of Adult Life in England. *447 pp.*
  2. Child-Rearing Practices and Index. *247 pp.*
Klein, Viola. The Feminine Character. *History of an Ideology. 244 pp.*
McWhinnie, Alexina M. Adopted Children. *How They Grow Up. 304 pp.*
● **Morgan, D. H. J.** Social Theory and the Family. *About 320 pp.*
● **Myrdal, Alva,** and **Klein, Viola.** Women's Two Roles: *Home and Work.* *238 pp. 27 tables.*
Parsons, Talcott, and **Bales, Robert F.** Family: Socialization and Inter-action Process. *In collaboration with James Olds, Morris Zelditch and Philip E. Slater. 456 pp. 50 figures and tables.*

SOCIAL SERVICES

Bastide, Roger. The Sociology of Mental Disorder. *Translated from the French by Jean McNeil. 260 pp.*
Carlebach, Julius. Caring For Children in Trouble. *266 pp.*
George, Victor. Foster Care. *Theory and Practice. 234 pp.*
  Social Security: *Beveridge and After. 258 pp.*
George, V., and **Wilding, P.** Motherless Families. *248 pp.*
●**Goetschius, George W.** Working with Community Groups. *256 pp.*
Goetschius, George W., and **Tash, Joan.** Working with Unattached Youth. *416 pp.*
Hall, M. P., and **Howes, I. V.** The Church in Social Work. *A Study of Moral Welfare Work undertaken by the Church of England. 320 pp.*
Heywood, Jean S. Children in Care: *the Development of the Service for the Deprived Child. 264 pp.*
Hoenig, J., and **Hamilton, Marian W.** The De-Segregation of the Mentally Ill. *284 pp.*
Jones, Kathleen. Mental Health and Social Policy, 1845-1959. *264 pp.*
King, Roy D., Raynes, Norma V., and **Tizard, Jack.** Patterns of Residential Care. *356 pp.*
Leigh, John. Young People and Leisure. *256 pp.*
●**Mays, John.** (Ed.) Penelope Hall's Social Services of England and Wales. *About 324 pp.*
Morris, Mary. Voluntary Work and the Welfare State. *300 pp.*
Nokes, P. L. The Professional Task in Welfare Practice. *152 pp.*
Timms, Noel. Psychiatric Social Work in Great Britain (1939-1962). *280 pp.*
● Social Casework: *Principles and Practice. 256 pp.*
Young, A. F. Social Services in British Industry. *272 pp.*

SOCIOLOGY OF EDUCATION

Banks, Olive. Parity and Prestige in English Secondary Education: a Study in Educational Sociology. *272 pp.*

Bentwich, Joseph. Education in Israel. *224 pp. 8 pp. plates.*

●**Blyth, W. A. L.** English Primary Education. *A Sociological Description.*
1. Schools. *232 pp.*
2. Background. *168 pp.*

Collier, K. G. The Social Purposes of Education: *Personal and Social Values in Education. 268 pp.*

Dale, R. R., and **Griffith, S.** Down Stream: *Failure in the Grammar School. 108 pp.*

Evans, K. M. Sociometry and Education. *158 pp.*

●**Ford, Julienne.** Social Class and the Comprehensive School. *192 pp.*

Foster, P. J. Education and Social Change in Ghana. *336 pp. 3 maps.*

Fraser, W. R. Education and Society in Modern France. *150 pp.*

Grace, Gerald R. Role Conflict and the Teacher. *150 pp.*

Hans, Nicholas. New Trends in Education in the Eighteenth Century. *278 pp. 19 tables.*

● Comparative Education: *A Study of Educational Factors and Traditions. 360 pp.*

●**Hargreaves, David.** Interpersonal Relations and Education. *432 pp.*

● Social Relations in a Secondary School. *240 pp.*

Holmes, Brian. Problems in Education. *A Comparative Approach. 336 pp.*

King, Ronald. Values and Involvement in a Grammar School. *164 pp.*

School Organization and Pupil Involvement. *A Study of Secondary Schools.*

●**Mannheim, Karl,** and **Stewart, W. A. C.** An Introduction to the Sociology of Education. *206 pp.*

Morris, Raymond N. The Sixth Form and College Entrance. *231 pp.*

●**Musgrove, F.** Youth and the Social Order. *176 pp.*

●**Ottaway, A. K. C.** Education and Society: An Introduction to the Sociology of Education. *With an Introduction by W. O. Lester Smith. 212 pp.*

Peers, Robert. Adult Education: *A Comparative Study. 398 pp.*

Pritchard, D. G. Education and the Handicapped: *1760 to 1960. 258 pp.*

Stratta, Erica. The Education of Borstal Boys. *A Study of their Educational Experiences prior to, and during, Borstal Training. 256 pp.*

Taylor, P. H., Reid, W. A., and **Holley, B. J.** The English Sixth Form. *A Case Study in Curriculum Research. 200 pp.*

SOCIOLOGY OF CULTURE

Eppel, E. M., and **M.** Adolescents and Morality: *A Study of some Moral Values and Dilemmas of Working Adolescents in the Context of a changing Climate of Opinion. Foreword by W. J. H. Sprott. 268 pp. 39 tables.*

●**Fromm, Erich.** The Fear of Freedom. *286 pp.*

● The Sane Society. *400 pp.*

Mannheim, Karl. Essays on the Sociology of Culture. *Edited by Ernst Mannheim in co-operation with Paul Kecskemeti. Editorial Note by Adolph Lowe. 280 pp.*

Weber, Alfred. Farewell to European History: *or The Conquest of Nihilism. Translated from the German by R. F. C. Hull. 224 pp.*

SOCIOLOGY OF RELIGION

Argyle, Michael and **Beit-Hallahmi, Benjamin.** The Social Psychology of Religion. *About 256 pp.*

Glasner, Peter E. The Sociology of Secularisation. *A Critique of a Concept. About 180 pp.*

Nelson, G. K. Spiritualism and Society. *313 pp.*

Stark, Werner. The Sociology of Religion. *A Study of Christendom.*
Volume I. *Established Religion. 248 pp.*
Volume II. *Sectarian Religion. 368 pp.*
Volume III. *The Universal Church. 464 pp.*
Volume IV. *Types of Religious Man. 352 pp.*
Volume V. *Types of Religious Culture. 464 pp.*

Turner, B. S. Weber and Islam. *216 pp.*

Watt, W. Montgomery. Islam and the Integration of Society. *320 pp.*

SOCIOLOGY OF ART AND LITERATURE

Jarvie, Ian C. Towards a Sociology of the Cinema. *A Comparative Essay on the Structure and Functioning of a Major Entertainment Industry. 405 pp.*

Rust, Frances S. Dance in Society. *An Analysis of the Relationships between the Social Dance and Society in England from the Middle Ages to the Present Day. 256 pp. 8 pp. of plates.*

Schücking, L. L. The Sociology of Literary Taste. *112 pp.*

Wolff, Janet. Hermeneutic Philosophy and the Sociology of Art. *150 pp.*

SOCIOLOGY OF KNOWLEDGE

Diesing, P. Patterns of Discovery in the Social Sciences. *262 pp.*

● **Douglas, J. D.** (Ed.) Understanding Everyday Life. *370 pp.*

● **Hamilton, P.** Knowledge and Social Structure. *174 pp.*

Jarvie, I. C. Concepts and Society. *232 pp.*

Mannheim, Karl. Essays on the Sociology of Knowledge. *Edited by Paul Kecskemeti. Editorial Note by Adolph Lowe. 353 pp.*

Remmling, Gunter W. The Sociology of Karl Mannheim. *With a Bibliographical Guide to the Sociology of Knowledge, Ideological Analysis, and Social Planning. 255 pp.*

Remmling, Gunter W. (Ed.) Towards the Sociology of Knowledge. *Origin and Development of a Sociological Thought Style. 463 pp.*

Stark, Werner. The Sociology of Knowledge: *An Essay in Aid of a Deeper Understanding of the History of Ideas. 384 pp.*

URBAN SOCIOLOGY

Ashworth, William. The Genesis of Modern British Town Planning: *A Study in Economic and Social History of the Nineteenth and Twentieth Centuries. 288 pp.*

Cullingworth, J. B. Housing Needs and Planning Policy: *A Restatement of the Problems of Housing Need and 'Overspill' in England and Wales. 232 pp. 44 tables. 8 maps.*

Dickinson, Robert E. City and Region: *A Geographical Interpretation 608 pp. 125 figures.*

The West European City: *A Geographical Interpretation. 600 pp. 129 maps. 29 plates.*

● The City Region in Western Europe. *320 pp. Maps.*

Humphreys, Alexander J. New Dubliners: *Urbanization and the Irish Family. Foreword by George C. Homans. 304 pp.*

Jackson, Brian. Working Class Community: *Some General Notions raised by a Series of Studies in Northern England. 192 pp.*

Jennings, Hilda. Societies in the Making: *a Study of Development and Re-development within a County Borough. Foreword by D. A. Clark. 286 pp.*

●**Mann, P. H.** An Approach to Urban Sociology. *240 pp.*

Morris, R. N., and **Mogey, J.** The Sociology of Housing. *Studies at Berinsfield. 232 pp. 4 pp. plates.*

Rosser, C., and **Harris, C.** The Family and Social Change. *A Study of Family and Kinship in a South Wales Town. 352 pp. 8 maps.*

●**Stacey, Margaret, Batsone, Eric, Bell, Colin,** and **Thurcott, Anne.** Power, Persistence and Change. *A Second Study of Banbury. 196 pp.*

RURAL SOCIOLOGY

Haswell, M. R. The Economics of Development in Village India. *120 pp.*

Littlejohn, James. Westrigg: *the Sociology of a Cheviot Parish. 172 pp. 5 figures.*

Mayer, Adrian C. Peasants in the Pacific. *A Study of Fiji Indian Rural Society. 248 pp. 20 plates.*

Williams, W. M. The Sociology of an English Village: *Gosforth. 272 pp. 12 figures. 13 tables.*

SOCIOLOGY OF INDUSTRY AND DISTRIBUTION

Anderson, Nels. Work and Leisure. *280 pp.*

●**Blau, Peter M.,** and **Scott, W. Richard.** Formal Organizations: *a Comparative approach. Introduction and Additional Bibliography by J. H. Smith. 326 pp.*

Dunkerley, David. The Foreman. *Aspects of Task and Structure. 192 pp.*

Eldridge, J. E. T. Industrial Disputes. *Essays in the Sociology of Industrial Relations. 288 pp.*

Hetzler, Stanley. Applied Measures for Promoting Technological Growth. *352 pp.*

Technological Growth and Social Change. *Achieving Modernization. 269 pp.*

Hollowell, Peter G. The Lorry Driver. *272 pp.*

●**Oxaal, I., Barnett, T.,** and **Booth, D.** (Eds). Beyond the Sociology of Development. *Economy and Society in Latin America and Africa. 295 pp.*

Smelser, Neil J. Social Change in the Industrial Revolution: *An Application of Theory to the Lancashire Cotton Industry, 1770–1840. 468 pp. 12 figures. 14 tables.*

ANTHROPOLOGY

Ammar, Hamed. Growing up in an Egyptian Village: *Silwa, Province of Aswan. 336 pp.*

Brandel-Syrier, Mia. Reeftown Elite. *A Study of Social Mobility in a Modern African Community on the Reef. 376 pp.*

Dickie-Clark, H. F. The Marginal Situation. *A Sociological Study of a Coloured Group. 236 pp.*

Dube, S. C. Indian Village. *Foreword by Morris Edward Opler. 276 pp. 4 plates.*

India's Changing Villages: *Human Factors in Community Development. 260 pp. 8 plates. 1 map.*

Firth, Raymond. Malay Fishermen. *Their Peasant Economy. 420 pp. 17 pp. plates.*

Gulliver, P. H. Social Control in an African Society: a Study of the Arusha, Agricultural Masai of Northern Tanganyika. *320 pp. 8 plates. 10 figures.*

Family Herds. *288 pp.*

Ishwaran, K. Tradition and Economy in Village India: *An Interactionist Approach. Foreword by Conrad Arensburg. 176 pp.*

Jarvie, Ian C. The Revolution in Anthropology. *268 pp.*

Little, Kenneth L. Mende of Sierra Leone. *308 pp. and folder.*

Negroes in Britain. *With a New Introduction and Contemporary Study by Leonard Bloom. 320 pp.*

Lowie, Robert H. Social Organization. *494 pp.*

Mayer, A. C. Peasants in the Pacific. *A Study of Fiji Indian Rural Society. 248 pp.*

Meer, Fatima. Race and Suicide in South Africa. *325 pp.*

Smith, Raymond T. The Negro Family in British Guiana: *Family Structure and Social Status in the Villages. With a Foreword by Meyer Fortes. 314 pp. 8 plates. 1 figure. 4 maps.*

Smooha, Sammy. Israel: Pluralism and Conflict. *About 320 pp.*

SOCIOLOGY AND PHILOSOPHY

Barnsley, John H. The Social Reality of Ethics. *A Comparative Analysis of Moral Codes. 448 pp.*

Diesing, Paul. Patterns of Discovery in the Social Sciences. *362 pp.*

●**Douglas, Jack D.** (Ed.) Understanding Everyday Life. *Toward the Reconstruction of Sociological Knowledge. Contributions by Alan F. Blum. Aaron W. Cicourel, Norman K. Denzin, Jack D. Douglas, John Heeren, Peter McHugh, Peter K. Manning, Melvin Power, Matthew Speier, Roy Turner, D. Lawrence Wieder, Thomas P. Wilson and Don H. Zimmerman. 370 pp.*

Gorman, Robert A. The Dual Vision. *Alfred Schutz and the Myth of Phenomenological Social Science. About 300 pp.*

Jarvie, Ian C. Concepts and Society. *216 pp.*

●**Pelz, Werner.** The Scope of Understanding in Sociology. *Towards a more radical reorientation in the social humanistic sciences. 283 pp.*

Roche, Maurice. Phenomenology, Language and the Social Sciences. *371 pp.*

Sahay, Arun. Sociological Analysis. *212 pp.*

Sklair, Leslie. The Sociology of Progress. *320 pp.*

Slater, P. Origin and Significance of the Frankfurt School. *A Marxist Perspective. About 192 pp.*

Smart, Barry. Sociology, Phenomenology and Marxian Analysis. *A Critical Discussion of the Theory and Practice of a Science of Society. 220 pp.*

International Library of Anthropology

General Editor Adam Kuper

Ahmed, A. S. Millenium and Charisma Among Pathans. *A Critical Essay in Social Anthropology. 192 pp.*

Brown, Paula. The Chimbu. *A Study of Change in the New Guinea Highlands. 151 pp.*

Gudeman, Stephen. Relationships, Residence and the Individual. *A Rural Panamanian Community. 288 pp. 11 Plates, 5 Figures, 2 Maps, 10 Tables.*

Hamnett, Ian. Chieftainship and Legitimacy. *An Anthropological Study of Executive Law in Lesotho. 163 pp.*

Hanson, F. Allan. Meaning in Culture. *127 pp.*

Lloyd, P. C. Power and Independence. *Urban Africans' Perception of Social Inequality. 264 pp.*

Pettigrew, Joyce. Robber Noblemen. *A Study of the Political System of the Sikh Jats. 284 pp.*
Street, Brian V. The Savage in Literature. *Representations of 'Primitive' Society in English Fiction, 1858–1920. 207 pp.*
Van Den Berghe, Pierre L. Power and Privilege at an African University. *278 pp.*

International Library of Social Policy

General Editor Kathleen Jones

Bayley, M. Mental Handicap and Community Care. *426 pp.*
Bottoms, A. E., and **McClean, J. D.** Defendants in the Criminal Process. *284 pp.*
Butler, J. R. Family Doctors and Public Policy. *208 pp.*
Davies, Martin. Prisoners of Society. *Attitudes and Aftercare. 204 pp.*
Gittus, Elizabeth. Flats, Families and the Under-Fives. *285 pp.*
Holman, Robert. Trading in Children. *A Study of Private Fostering. 355 pp.*
Jones, Howard, and **Cornes, Paul.** Open Prisons. *About 248 pp.*
Jones, Kathleen. History of the Mental Health Service. *428 pp.*
Jones, Kathleen, with **Brown, John, Cunningham, W. J., Roberts, Julian,** and **Williams, Peter.** Opening the Door. *A Study of New Policies for the Mentally Handicapped. 278 pp.*
Karn, Valerie. Retiring to the Seaside. *About 280 pp. 2 maps. Numerous tables.*
Thomas, J. E. The English Prison Officer since 1850: *A Study in Conflict. 258 pp.*
Walton, R. G. Women in Social Work. *303 pp.*
Woodward, J. To Do the Sick No Harm. *A Study of the British Voluntary Hospital System to 1875. 221 pp.*

International Library of Welfare and Philosophy

General Editors Noel Timms and David Watson

● **Plant, Raymond.** Community and Ideology. *104 pp.*

● **McDermott, F. E.** (Ed.) Self-Determination in Social Work. *A Collection of Essays on Self-determination and Related Concepts by Philosophers and Social Work Theorists. Contributors: F. P. Biestek, S. Bernstein, A. Keith-Lucas, D. Sayer, H. H. Perelman, C. Whittington, R. F. Stalley, F. E. McDermott, I. Berlin, H. J. McCloskey, H. L. A. Hart, J. Wilson, A. I. Melden, S. I. Benn. 254 pp.*
Ragg, Nicholas M. People Not Cases. *A Philosophical Approach to Social Work. About 250 pp.*

● **Timms, Noel,** and **Watson, David** (Eds). Talking About Welfare. *Readings in Philosophy and Social Policy. Contributors: T. H. Marshall, R. B. Brandt, G. H. von Wright, K. Nielsen, M. Cranston, R. M. Titmuss, R. S. Downie, E. Telfer, D. Donnison, J. Benson, P. Leonard, A. Keith-Lucas, D. Walsh, I. T. Ramsey. 320 pp.*

Primary Socialization, Language and Education

General Editor Basil Bernstein

Adlam, Diana S., *with the assistance of Geoffrey Turner and Lesley Lineker.* Code in Context. *About 272 pp.*

Bernstein, Basil. Class, Codes and Control. *3 volumes.*
 1. *Theoretical Studies Towards a Sociology of Language. 254 pp.*
 2. *Applied Studies Towards a Sociology of Language. 377 pp.*
● 3. *Towards a Theory of Educatiomal Transmission. 167 pp.*

Brandis, W., and **Bernstein, B.** Selection and Control. *176 pp.*

Brandis, Walter, and **Henderson, Dorothy.** Social Class, Language and Communication. *288 pp.*

Cook-Gumperz, Jenny. Social Control and Socialization. *A Study of Class Differences in the Language of Maternal Control. 290 pp.*

●**Gahagan, D. M.,** and **G. A.** Talk Reform. *Exploration in Language for Infant School Children. 160 pp.*

Hawkins, P. R. Social Class, the Nominal Group and Verbal Strategies. *About 220 pp.*

Robinson, W. P., and **Rackstraw, Susan D. A.** A Question of Answers. *2 volumes. 192 pp. and 180 pp.*

Turner, Geoffrey J., and **Mohan, Bernard A.** A Linguistic Description and Computer Programme for Children's Speech. *208 pp.*

Reports of the Institute of Community Studies

●**Cartwright, Ann.** Parents and Family Planning Services. *306 pp.*
 Patients and their Doctors. *A Study of General Practice. 304 pp.*

Dench, Geoff. Maltese in London. *A Case-study in the Erosion of Ethnic Consciousness. 302 pp.*

●**Jackson, Brian.** Streaming: *an Education System in Miniature. 168 pp.*

Jackson, Brian, and **Marsden, Dennis.** Education and the Working Class: *Some General Themes raised by a Study of 88 Working-class Children in a Northern Industrial City. 268 pp. 2 folders.*

Marris, Peter. The Experience of Higher Education. *232 pp. 27 tables.*
 Loss and Change. *192 pp.*

Marris, Peter, and **Rein, Martin.** Dilemmas of Social Reform. *Poverty and Community Action in the United States. 256 pp.*

Marris, Peter, and Somerset, Anthony. African Businessmen. *A Study of Entrepreneurship and Development in Kenya. 256 pp.*

Mills, Richard. Young Outsiders: *a Study in Alternative Communities. 216 pp.*

Runciman, W. G. Relative Deprivation and Social Justice. *A Study of Attitudes to Social Inequality in Twentieth-Century England. 352 pp.*

Willmott, Peter. Adolescent Boys in East London. *230 pp.*

Willmott, Peter, and Young, Michael. Family and Class in a London Suburb. *202 pp. 47 tables.*

Young, Michael. Innovation and Research in Education. *192 pp.*

●Young, Michael, and McGeeney, Patrick. Learning Begins at Home. *A Study of a Junior School and its Parents. 128 pp.*

Young, Michael, and Willmott, Peter. Family and Kinship in East London. *Foreword by Richard M. Titmuss. 252 pp. 39 tables.*

The Symmetrical Family. *410 pp.*

Reports of the Institute for Social Studies in Medical Care

Cartwright, Ann, Hockey, Lisbeth, and Anderson, John L. Life Before Death. *310 pp.*

Dunnell, Karen, and Cartwright, Ann. Medicine Takers, Prescribers and Hoarders. *190 pp.*

Medicine, Illness and Society

General Editor W. M. Williams

Robinson, David. The Process of Becoming Ill. *142 pp.*

Stacey, Margaret, *et al.* Hospitals, Children and Their Families. *The Report of a Pilot Study. 202 pp.*

Stimson, G. V., and Webb, B. Going to See the Doctor. *The Consultation Process in General Practice. 155 pp.*

Monographs in Social Theory

General Editor Arthur Brittan

●Barnes, B. Scientific Knowledge and Sociological Theory. *192 pp.*

Bauman, Zygmunt. Culture as Praxis. *204 pp.*

●Dixon, Keith. Sociological Theory. *Pretence and Possibility. 142 pp.*

Meltzer, B. N., Petras, J. W., and Reynolds, L. T. Symbolic Interactionism. *Genesis, Varieties and Criticisms. 144 pp.*

●Smith, Anthony D. The Concept of Social Change. *A Critique of the Functionalist Theory of Social Change. 208 pp.*

Routledge Social Science Journals

The British Journal of Sociology. *Editor – Angus Stewart; Associate Editor – Leslie Sklair. Vol. 1, No. 1 – March 1950 and Quarterly. Roy. 8vo. All back issues available. An international journal publishing original papers in the field of sociology and related areas.*
Community Work. *Edited by David Jones and Marjorie Mayo. 1973. Published annually.*
Economy and Society. *Vol. 1, No. 1. February 1972 and Quarterly. Metric Roy. 8vo. A journal for all social scientists covering sociology, philosophy, anthropology, economics and history. All back numbers available.*
Religion. Journal of Religion and Religions. *Chairman of Editorial Board, Ninian Smart. Vol. 1, No. 1, Spring 1971. A journal with an interdisciplinary approach to the study of the phenomena of religion. All back numbers available.*
Year Book of Social Policy in Britain, The. *Edited by Kathleen Jones. 1971. Published annually.*

Social and Psychological Aspects of Medical Practice

Editor   Trevor Silverstone

Lader, Malcolm. Psychophysiology of Mental Illness. *280 pp.*
● **Silverstone, Trevor,** and **Turner, Paul.** Drug Treatment in Psychiatry. *232 pp.*

Printed in Great Britain by
Lowe & Brydone Printers Limited, Thetford, Norfolk